RIVERS IN WORLD HISTORY

The Indus River

The Rio Grande

The St. Lawrence River

The Tigris and Euphrates Rivers

The Volga River

The Yukon River

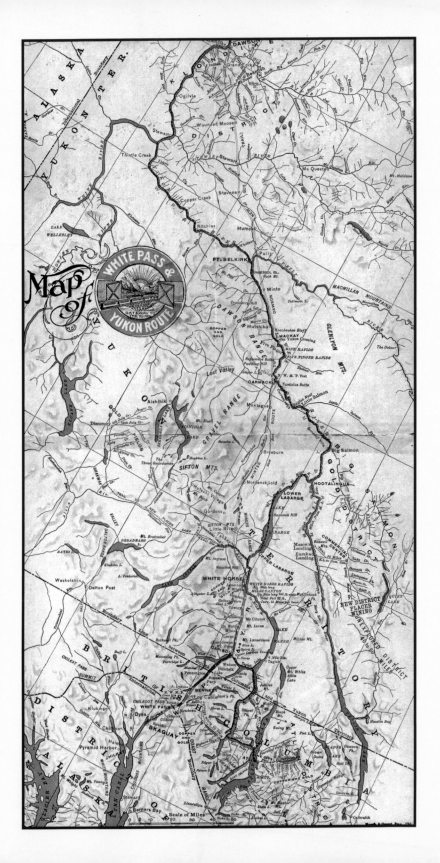

THE YUKON RIVER

Tim McNeese

CHELSEA HOUSE
PUBLISHERS
A Haights Cross Communications Company
Philadelphia

FRONTIS: Map of the route of the White Pass and Yukon Railroad through Yukon Territory, Canada. The Yukon River runs through the center of the map, starting at Dawson at the top-center.

CHELSEA HOUSE PUBLISHERS

VP, NEW PRODUCT DEVELOPMENT Sally Cheney
DIRECTOR OF PRODUCTION Kim Shinners
CREATIVE MANAGER Takeshi Takahashi
MANUFACTURING MANAGER Diann Grasse

Staff for THE YUKON RIVER

EXECUTIVE EDITOR Lee Marcott
EDITOR Christian Green
PRODUCTION EDITOR Noelle Nardone
PHOTO EDITOR Sarah Bloom
SERIES AND COVER DESIGNER Keith Trego
LAYOUT 21st Century Publishing and Communications, Inc.

A Haights Cross Communications ✦ Company

First Printing

9 8 7 6 5 4 3 2 1

Library of Congress Cataloging-in-Publication Data

McNeese, Tim.
   The Yukon River / Tim McNeese
      p. cm.—(Rivers in world history)
Includes bibliographical references and index.
   ISBN 0-7910-8248-2 (hardcover)
   1. Yukon River (Yukon and Alaska)—Juvenile literature. 2. Yukon River Valley
(Yukon and Alaska)—Juvenile literature. 3. Yukon River (Yukon and Alaska)—
History—Juvenile literature. 4. Yukon River Valley (Yukon and Alaska)—History—
Juvenile literature. I. Title II. Series.
F912.Y9M38 2005
979.8'6—dc22

                                                                                          2004022016

All links and Web addresses were checked and verified to be correct at the time of publication. Because of the dynamic nature of the Web, some addresses and links may have changed since publication and may no longer be valid.

CONTENTS

1

The Great
Northern River

This arctic artery of the north, the Yukon River, was named by its earliest inhabitants, the Inuits, commonly known as the Eskimos. They used an Athapaskan word, *yukonna*, a name that translates as "great river." It is, indeed, a lengthy, winding river, carrying a mighty flow. Charted at nearly 2,300 miles long from its Canadian headwaters in British Columbia, the Yukon River arcs into Alaska, crossing America's largest state along a twisting course until it empties into the icy waters of the Bering Sea. Just over half its course, approximately 1,260 miles, flows through Alaska. It ranks as the seventeenth longest river in the world and the seventh longest in the entire Western Hemisphere. The Yukon is longer than other notable American waterways, including the Colorado, the Columbia, and the Rio Grande. Only four rivers in North America—the Mississippi, the Missouri, the Arkansas, and the Ohio—are longer.

The length of the Yukon, however, only begins to define the river's significance. Other features of the river are as prominent as the open, wilderness landscape the Yukon passes through. The river drains an enormous region, an area estimated at 300,000 square miles. Alaska has more water than any other American state, and its landscape is crisscrossed with 3,000 rivers and lesser streams. In such a significant watershed, the Yukon River delivers great amounts of water, making it the fifth greatest in water flow in the world. Only the Amazon, the Mississippi, the Missouri, and the St. Lawrence, another Canadian river far to the east, carry more water.

The Yukon is one of the United States' most unique river systems. Unlike its counterparts in the lower 48 states, this Canadian-U.S. waterway is not home to millions of residents who live within close proximity of its banks. It features no major dam or impoundment system. Every major river in the United States, from the Mississippi to the Missouri to the Ohio to the Columbia, features multiple dam systems. The Yukon is not dotted by urban centers or major cityscapes. There is only one major bridge—constructed in 1975— that crosses the Yukon: it is located on the Dalton Highway, a road built to provide access to the oil fields along the North Slope of Alaska and to extend the Trans-Alaska Oil Pipeline across the river. The Yukon is nearly pristine, largely untouched and not impacted by human elements such as pollution. No major transportation system parallels extensive stretches of the Yukon, such as highway or rail systems. In addition, the environment through which the Yukon passes is unlike any other in the United States. Over much of its length, the river follows its natural tendencies— its path unaltered by humans, "its channels and banks shift constantly, aided by annual floods caused by ice jams during spring breakup."[1] Running as far north as the Arctic Circle, the Yukon is not navigable during much of an average year. Shallow draft boats, however, first built in 1975, can navigate nearly all the river's course during the summer months, from June to September.

Although this great northern river is different in many ways from its American counterparts, the Yukon River is still a waterway of extraordinary beauty and mystery, a river tucked away in an environment that discourages human occupation. Today, few people populate the course of the Yukon, thus allowing the river to continue largely unspoiled, untamed, and untapped in its natural cycle; one it has followed for tens of thousands of years. Yet, even though the area around the river is home to few human inhabitants, it flows through a northern wilderness abundant with wildlife. Great herds of reindeer, together with mink, lynx, marten, wolverines, elk, and the great hunter of the north—the grizzly bear—drink from its crystal waters.

The Yukon is a river of several origins. Deep within the jagged, rocky mountains of British Columbia, in northwestern Canada, sits Teslin Lake, 85 miles long and one of the Yukon's major sources. This remote, serene, freshwater lake provides the water for the Teslin River, which flows out of the lake's northern

An aerial view of Eagle, Alaska—the first town the Yukon River passes by after it crosses the border between Yukon Territory and Alaska. Eagle was founded in 1897 and was a supply and trading center for miners.

end. As the Teslin flows through thick forests of mountain timber, it is joined by the Big Salmon River, flowing in from the east. Together, the Teslin and Big Salmon Rivers provide the waters for the Lewes River, which is actually the headwaters of the Yukon River. These rivers receive water from hundreds of thousands of acres of Yukon wilderness.

Along this leg of the river, the Upper Yukon stretches 300 yards from bank to bank. Its waters are frigid, clear, and typically shallow. The Lewes portion of the river is pristine, nearly unspoiled by any human pollution. Here, the most important community is Whitehorse, the remote capital of Canada's Yukon Territory. Whitehorse is now home to approximately three of every four of the Yukon Territory's 25,000 residents. It is at Whitehorse that most practical navigation of the Yukon begins. Downriver from Whitehorse, the Yukon is fed by another of its water sources, a major tributary called the Pelly River. It was named during the 1840s by one of the first white men to reach its banks, Robert Campbell, a fur trader for the Hudson's Bay Company. Campbell named the Pelly after the fur company's owner. It was here at the confluence of the Pelly and the Upper Yukon that Campbell and his colleagues erected a trading post, Fort Selkirk. Today, the site is a Native American settlement.

Below Fort Selkirk, the Yukon takes on an additional tributary source, the White River, which flows in from the west as it tumbles out of the Wrangell Mountains. The White River is appropriately named, for its waters are thick with whitish silt from the giant glaciers of the St. Elias Range. Here, the crystalline waters of the Upper Yukon are tainted by the silty White. For the remainder of the Yukon's course, its waters remain muddy, until it reaches the Bering Sea. Farther down-river, yet another major tributary adds to the flow of the Yukon. The Stewart River, named for a colleague of Robert Campbell, flows from the east and reaches the Yukon about 100 miles south of the town of Dawson. This length of the Yukon River is dotted with many small, tree-covered islands. The area's wildlife, including black bear and moose, feed along the hilly banks that flank the river.

Farther on, the Yukon River is fed by yet another tributary, this one flowing in from the west and oddly named the Sixtymile River. This feeder river was named during the 1870s after the construction of Fort Reliance, a trading post on the Yukon, located about six miles downriver from the confluence of the

Klondike and Yukon. With no other settlements for hundreds of miles, local trappers and prospectors named local rivers according to the distance from Fort Reliance. Situated approximately 60 miles upriver from the post, this tributary of the Yukon was thus named for its distance from Fort Reliance. (The Fortymile River, downriver from Fort Reliance by the same distance, was also named in this way, as were other such rivers as the Fifteenmile and the Seventymile.)

Farther downriver, the Yukon slips through a series of narrows, only to reach the confluence of its largest tributary river, the western-flowing Klondike. At this great arctic river crossroads, the city of Dawson still stands, its buildings and old steamboat wharves reminiscent of the great gold rush of the late 1890s. Between 1896 and 1898, Dawson City was the raucous home of nearly 40,000 gold seekers, making the remote wilderness town the largest west of the Canadian city of Winnipeg. Today, Dawson is home to 2,000 permanent residents and remains a popular tourist attraction for tens of thousands of visitors annually.

With the added flow of the Klondike, the Yukon continues its generally northern course, reaching a much smaller tributary, Fortymile—another important historical site connected to the gold rush of the 1890s. A feeder river to Fortymile is the Chicken River, so named by late-nineteenth-century prospectors who discovered gold nuggets the size of chicken feed. Just below Fortymile, the Yukon River crosses from one country to another as it leaves Canada and enters the state of Alaska. The first Alaskan village on the Yukon is Eagle, a tiny community once visited in 1905 by the great Norwegian polar explorer, Roald Amundsen, who had just sailed a ship from the Atlantic to the Pacific through the Northwest Passage, a route that had eluded explorers for four centuries. From Eagle, Amundsen sent a cable by military wireless to Norway announcing his successful adventure.

Roald Amundsen, a Norwegian explorer, was the first person to negotiate the Northwest Passage—the northern route that links the Atlantic and Pacific Oceans—when he commanded the *Gjöa* through the region from 1903 to 1906. After accomplishing the feat, Amundsen stopped in Eagle, Alaska, to wire the Norwegian government of his success.

As the Yukon continues past Eagle, it moves into one of its most spectacular legs, the 180-mile stretch from Eagle to Circle, Alaska. In *The Yukon*, Marian T. Place described this portion of the Yukon's course:

> Each bend in the river brings towering mountains into view. The sharp peaks of the Sheep Mountains dominate the countryside.

At any point along here it is not unusual to see bear, caribou, moose, beaver, muskrat, and marten. The mountain sheep on the heights usually have to be viewed through binoculars.[2]

As the river reaches Circle, it reconnects with its gold rush days. Established in 1893 by Leroy "Jack" McQuesten, who also founded Fort Reliance, the town was so named because McQuesten believed he had reached the Arctic Circle, not realizing he was still 50 miles south of the polar line. Thousands came to Circle in search of gold a century ago, but today the settlement is a small Inuit village of several dozen residents. Circle is also noteworthy as the northernmost site connected to the U.S. Interstate Highway System.

As Circle marks the end of one of the most beautiful segments of the river, so the landscape beyond the tiny Indian settlement changes. Mountains that flanked the river recede into the distance as the river passes through the Yukon Flats. Here, the low-lying landscape allows the Yukon to meander from its typically single channel. The river moves through the next 60 miles across changing channels and winding banks as a number of options for navigation present themselves. Despite the opportunity for the Yukon to spread itself out across the flats, the river's course remains swift, helping cut additional silt away from its bank and causing the river to become extremely thick and dirty. The land along the river is nearly barren, marked by thin spruce and willow stands. River banks cave in constantly, shifting the main channel of the river. As one early European arrival to this portion of the Yukon noted, in 1847, "I never saw an uglier river."[3]

Nearly 90 miles beyond the Yukon Flats, the river finally reaches its northernmost point, arriving at the Arctic Circle, where winter temperatures can plummet more than 60 to 70 degrees below zero. At this farthest northern reach of the Yukon, the river takes a sudden turn to the southwest, completing the river's long arc from its source in southwestern Yukon Territory. The town of Fort Yukon, the oldest English-speaking settlement on the Yukon, is the only important community on this portion of the river. The settlement is so remote that it can only be reached by boat, plane, or dogsled. Several hundred citizens continue to call Fort Yukon home, despite the isolation they experience through much of an average year. The ground flanking this leg of the Yukon is permafrost, its subsurface frozen permanently, allowing ground water to only penetrate a few inches of topsoil. With water unable to drain adequately in this region, the Yukon here runs parallel to an endless number of tiny lakes and swamps, where mosquitoes breed in great numbers in the summer.

From Fort Yukon, the river continues to follow a new, south-westerly course, through 175 additional miles of flats. The river finally arrives at a mountain chain, though, and slips through a narrow pass as it becomes a single channel again. During the 1960s, the U.S. Army Corps of Engineers fought hard for the construction of a massive dam project on this portion of the Yukon. The Rampart Dam would have stood more than 500 feet in height and impounded enough water to create a lake larger than Lake Erie, extending upriver to Circle. The lake might have provided a summer habitat for 1.5 million migratory birds. The dam's hydroelectric facility would have been capable of generating 8 billion kilowatt-hours of electricity annually. Because of a lack of support and economic justification, however, the dam was never constructed.

Yet another major river links up with the Yukon beyond the flats, the second longest river in Alaska—the Tanana. This major tributary increases the flow of the Yukon as it continues its course toward the Bering Sea, and the great Alaskan river broadens extensively. Other waters lie ahead, including the Melozitna tributary, where snowy mountains rise above the river. Passing another old mining community, Ruby, the Yukon flows through still another monotonous run of flats and another tributary, the Koyukuk River, which reaches the Yukon from the north.

On its final leg before reaching the sea, the Yukon arrives at Nulato, 20 miles downriver from the Koyukuk confluence. The first European settlement was established here on the river during the 1830s by employees of the Russian Fur Company. The Russians erected a fort and trading post, only to have the original site burned by local Native Americans. Over the next 15 years, the Russians built and rebuilt Nulato several times over following various Indian raids, burnings, and massacres. Today, Nulato still exists as an Indian community of a few hundred residents, the Russians are gone, and the village is supplied by regular airplane deliveries.

Although another Indian settlement is located 40 miles downstream from Nulato, a village called Kaltag, the river flows for another 160 miles before reaching another inhabited site, the village of Anvik, situated along the Anvik River, also a Yukon tributary. At Anvik, the Native American population engages heavily in the salmon trade. The town is home to fewer than 100 residents, 9 out of 10 of whom are of Alaskan Indian ancestry. Here, the Yukon has flowed across western Canada and much of Alaska for 2,000 miles, but the river still remains 300 miles from its mouth along the Bering Sea.

This final portion of the Yukon's course is uninspiring, consisting of still more flats as the river turns to the northwest. Swamps again mark the region around the river until the Yukon finally reaches the Bering Sea south of Norton Sound, "an utterly wild and bleak spot, depressing to many, and far removed from civilization."[4] For miles beyond the mouth of the Yukon, its dark, silty waters slip out into the cold, blue water of the Bering Sea, clouding the sea flow. Dozens of rivers have fed its course over 2,300 miles, only to reach yet another remote corner of Alaskan wilderness, unseen by any humans, with the exception of an occasional Inuit fishing party.

THE ANCIENT ORIGINS OF THE YUKON

The beginnings of the Yukon River are shrouded in the mists of geologic time, when the landscape of modern-day Alaska was inundated beneath a warm-water sea. As the sea receded, the landscape remained warmer than today, and vegetation was thick and varied. According to modern geologists, "fifty million years ago magnolia and fig trees grew in Alaska, along with giant redwoods, chestnuts, and elms."[5] This prolonged "hothouse" period of Alaskan history eventually subsided, however, and the northern region began to turn colder and wetter. The vegetation died out and great, snowy arctic winters arrived. Alaska and the lands spanned by the Yukon River faced endless cold, with mounting snows that created great ice fields.

About one million years B.P. ("before present"), these immense ice sheets began to move and shift across the region of northwestern Canada and Alaska. In some places, ice accumulated to a depth of two miles. Over hundreds of thousands of years, the ice fields moved, buckling the earth's surface and scarring the landscape. Great mountains were thrust up and deep, glacial valleys were formed, including the valleys that today constitute the Yukon River system. Eventually, much of Alaska lost its permanent glacial ice cover. There were exposed patches of green pasturelands, which attracted the great Pleistocene animals, such as mastodons, with their huge, curving tusks and the shaggy, thick-skinned, woolly mammoths.

Many of these animals wandered into the Alaskan region from what is now Siberia, where the great ice sheets had not completely receded. Though extensive regions of the Siberian north were still locked in ice, a land bridge developed between the farthest reaches of Russia and the Alaskan coast due to receding waters. Approximately 20,000 years ago, the land bridge was extensive enough to allow large numbers of animals to migrate into the Western Hemisphere.

At that time, Alaska was a relative paradise of the north. The attractiveness of the region drew not only large herds of animals but also humans, perhaps the first to reach the Western Hemisphere. Soon, two migrations took place simultaneously:

> By this time the land we call Alaska was covered with dense growth of small spruce and other evergreens, and tough grass. The great beasts fed on this. They had few enemies until men appeared on the scene, also about twenty thousand years ago. They, too, came from Asia across the land bridge onto America. In small groups these wandering nomads hunted the mastodons and mammoths for their hides and meat.[6]

Humans moved into Alaska from Asia over several thousands of years, not in one massive migratory movement. (These primitive, nomadic hunters never realized they had moved from one continent to another.) Of those ancient peoples who made their way into the New World, modern anthropologists identify four ethnic groups, including the Inuit, or Eskimos, who settled along the Bering and Arctic coastlands; the Athapaskans, who migrated and settled in the interior of Alaska; the Aleuts, who took up residence on the Aleutian Islands extending out into the Pacific from southwestern Alaska; and the Tlingit-Haida Indians, who reached the southern and southeastern coastal regions of Alaska. Only two of these four migratory groups—the Inuits and the Athapaskans—made extensive and important connections with the Yukon River. Over time, the massive land bridge linking Siberia and Alaska was submerged under water, and the opportunity for Asiatic peoples to reach the lands of Alaska became more difficult. With these earlier migrations, though, the human history of the Yukon River had begun.

2

The People
of the River

For thousands of years, Asiatic peoples migrated unwittingly from one continent to another, from the Old World to the New. Multiple migrations from different eras saw the arrival of several groups of Asians to the Western Hemisphere. Of the four primary groups of origin, only two—the Inuits (Eskimos) and the Athapaskans—settled in significant numbers in the region of the Yukon River. Ethnologists and others who identify Native American cultural groups usually identify these Indian migrants as belonging to the Subarctic Cultural Group. The group's regional origin, however, is much larger than that of those who settled in Alaska or Canada's Yukon Territory. The region included as *subarctic* "stretches across North America south of the Arctic from interior Alaska and the Canadian Rockies to Labrador and Newfoundland." [7] This extensive area includes not only Alaska but Canada from its western territories east to the Atlantic Ocean. Those Native Americans who lived in this culture group existed in a harsh environment in which the temperatures were extreme, ranging from 80 degrees below zero in the winter to 100 degrees in summer. For those living in the region of the Yukon River, their world was one of challenges, as well as of natural rewards.

THE ATHAPASKANS

As modern linguists attempt to categorize various Native American cultural groups in Alaska and Canada, they divide the subarctic tribes into two major language families, the Algonquians and the Athapaskans. The Athapaskans have lived for thousands of years west of Hudson Bay and west across Alaska. The name "Athapaskan" comes from a single band of Native Americans who lived along the banks of Lake Athabasca in northwestern Canada.

These Athapaskan-speaking Indians lived along the great basin lands of the Yukon and Mackenzie Rivers and along other streams and rivers in the Yukon Territory and Alaska that

The Inuits, or Eskimos, and the Athapaskans are the two primary Native American groups who historically inhabited the Yukon River region. Shown here is an Inuit woman stringing cod to be dried.

empty into the Arctic and Pacific Oceans, as well as the Gulf of Alaska. Although other groups existed among their number, those who lived along the Yukon or nearby included the Hans, found on the Upper Yukon in East-Central Alaska and the western Yukon Territory; the Ingaliks, who made their homes along the Lower Yukon River; the Koyukons, who lived in the Yukon Basin in Alaska; the Kutchins, those who occupied lands extending from Alaska's Upper Yukon Valley, across the central region of Yukon Territory, and down the Lower Mackenzie River; the Tananas, situated at the confluence of the Yukon and Tanana Rivers in Alaska; and the Tutchones, in the southern Yukon Territory.

Compared to the Algonquians, the Athapaskans are thought by anthropologists to have reached the New World later, with the vanguard reaching Alaska from northeastern Asia between 3,000 and 4,000 B.C. Some experts estimate their earliest arrival as far back as 6,000 B.C. Regardless, through the centuries following their arrival in the New World, the Athapaskans appeared intent on continuing their migration south, "possibly seeking more hospitable country where winters were not so long or severe."[8] At some distant point in the past, the Athapaskans who remained in the subarctic split off with another group, who continued their migration south. The language native to many Athapaskans, part of the Na-Dene linguistic stock, is part of the same language group spoken today by the Navajos and Apaches, who live thousands of miles to the south in the American Southwest regions of Arizona and New Mexico.

As early residents of the subarctic regions of Alaska and Canada, the Athapaskans did not practice systematic agriculture. Their men were typically hunters and fishers—it was probably the migratory Pleistocene animals that had originally lured them across the Bering Land Bridge. The wildlife they found along the Yukon River was ample and abundant. A wide range of animal prey, large and small, could be counted on, including moose, elk, bear, caribou, musk oxen, beaver, porcupine, and rabbit. The Athapaskans relied heavily on the caribou and it became "as important to Alaska's Athapaskans as bison were to southern Plains Indians."[9] The hunters used various simple weapons, including bows and arrows, clubs, spears, and several types of snares. One tribal group of Athapaskans, the Sekanis, fashioned a club from the jawbone of a moose. Some tribal groups preferred to rely on fishing over hunting. Throughout history, the Athapaskans have been known "for exceptional strength, resourcefulness, and stamina."[10]

THE INGALIKS

Among the Athapaskans, the Ingaliks form one of the dominant culture groups of the modern Yukon-based tribes. For hundreds and perhaps thousands of years, the Ingaliks have lived in the territory flanking the banks of such rivers as the Anvik, Innoko, Holitna, and Lower Yukon and have shared these homelands with the Kuskowagamiut Inuits. Ethnologists use the name "Ingalik" to refer to several separate, yet culturally similar tribes in the region, including the Koyukon, Tanana, and Han. The word *ingalik* is derived from the Russian interpretation of an Inuit word for "Indian." The numbers of Ingaliks have remained small in more modern times. Perhaps 1,500 lived in the Alaska-Yukon subarctic region during the nineteenth century; today, they number fewer than 700.

The Ingaliks have often lived in isolation, remaining to themselves and seldom engaging in conflicts or war with neighboring tribal groups. When they did fight, it was most often with the Koyukon or other Athapaskan tribes. They did not trade extensively with their neighbors because the Ingaliks lived in rich valleys with abundant natural resources. When they did trade, it was often with the Inuits. The exchange might often have included Ingalik wooden bowls, furs, wolverine hides, and birch bark canoes traded for Inuit fish, seal products, and caribou hides, as well as tooth shells called dentalia.

The Ingaliks practiced traditional Indian arts, including the fashioning of bark canoes, wooden sleds, and snowshoes and baskets made of either animal hides or bark, such as birch or willow. Their weapons included bows and arrows and spears. They made tools and utilitarian items from stone, bone, horn, or wood, including wood knives, wooden bowls, stone axes and wedges, fish traps, and snares. They made their clothing from squirrel and other skins. Both men and women wore shirts and pants as well as parkas to protect them from the subarctic winters. Women's pants often had the moccasins attached to them. The

Ingaliks enjoyed personal decoration, and they wore necklaces, nose piercings, and dentalium earrings. They also fringed their buckskin clothing, used porcupine quills to embellish clothing and hairstyles, and the women, following European contact, became respected for their beautiful beadwork.

These people of the Yukon River lived in summer and winter villages, as well as more temporary canoe or spring camps. Their winter houses were built partially underground to help retain heat, were dome-shaped and covered over with various grasses and earth, and provided living space for as many as three nuclear families. A typical Ingalik winter encampment might include a dozen houses. A communal building was often featured in such dwelling sites—a larger, rectangular communal facility, built partially in the ground, and used by the men of the village. Along the sides of the large hut, called a *kashim*, were the canoes and sleds used by the men. Inside, the Ingalik men practiced special ceremonies, including ritualistic "sweats," ate, worked, and slept.

During the warmer months, the Ingalik groups erected summer houses built of spruce plank, spruce bark, or cottonwood logs. These buildings and homes were airy, lighter, and easily collapsible, allowing their occupants to move them from place to place. Such summer villages often featured gable-roofed smokehouses, where fish could be dried and later stored for winter consumption. The Ingaliks built a canoe camp when they were engaged in a prolonged fishing expedition. The camps included "cone-shaped spruce-pole and bough shelters."[11] Although the Ingaliks tended to remain indoors during the winter months, they were sometimes highly mobile during the summer, relying on their birch bark canoes to carry them and their household items up and down such rivers as the Yukon, the Anvik, the Koyukuk, and the Tanana.

Fish was the most important part of the Ingalik diet. It gave their meals much variety because they caught many types, including trout, whitefish, pike, blackfish, and, the most highly prized of them all, salmon. Hunters provided many different types of wild meat. The Ingaliks were known to have engaged in communal hunting, which involved surrounding large prey, such as caribou—one of their favorite meats. The hunted animals "were driven into staked barriers equipped with snares, or funneled into corrals where 20 hunters could kill hundreds of animals—several months' supply of food, skins, horn, and bones."[12] They supplemented their meals with birds, including the abundant waterfowl of the region, and bird eggs. They also gathered plants, seeds, and berries. The Ingaliks had a special food, a form of ice cream that was concocted from cottonwood pods, oil, snow, and berries, which they ate during important ceremonies.

The Ingalik social structure recognized different classes among its people, who were ranked by status. The identified classes included the wealthy, the common people, and the "idlers." Those who possessed greater wealth were expected to share with others, give gifts, and host elaborate giving ceremonies called potlatches. A potlatch was an opportunity for wealth redistribution by a host who owned abundant furs, quantities of dried fish, animal meat, and other goods, such as carved bowls, drums, or even a canoe. The host held a large feast and made great ceremony of giving away a portion of the wealth. Those of the poorest class, the idlers, were considered of low status and commonly considered "unmarriageable," because they would bring no wealth or status to a marriage. The class was not a caste, however, and one born into the idler class could move up. (For additional information on these Native feasts, enter "potlatch cermony" into any search engine and browse the many sites listed.)

Ingaliks did not always marry exclusively within their own tribal group. They would marry outside their village and interrelated family groups, even to the point of marrying among their Inuit neighbors. A young woman was considered of marrying age when she had completed passage through puberty. At the first sign of adolescence, such a young girl was expected to live in isolation from men for a year, during which time she was taught all the skills of keeping a household and caring for children. Marriages sometimes included multiple wives, but a man was expected to receive permission from his first wife before he took a second. A man who claimed two wives first had to have enough wealth to sustain such a complex household.

Religious practices among the Ingaliks included the nearly universal concept of a spirit existing inside everything, from a rock to the moon. It did not matter whether a thing was alive or inanimate. In the Ingalik cosmic mind-set, the world and the universe consisted of four levels, which included one higher, two lower, and Earth. These worlds were occupied by a Creator spirit; other spirits associated with the natural world; additional special spirits and lesser deities, including superhuman beings; and people themselves. The spirits of the dead could travel to any of the four worlds, depending on the nature or method of the death. As with other Athapaskan tribes, the Ingalik relied on special priests, the shamans, who could be either male or female. Such holy individuals were shrouded in mystery, knew special rituals and songs, and were expected to heal people and predict the future. Shamans were capable of doing both good and harm—some of their special songs were intended to place a curse or hex on their victim.

It was important to the Ingaliks to maintain a harmony between these various spirit worlds in the cosmos. They carried out many rituals and ceremonies with that purpose in mind; these included a two- to three-week Animals ceremony, the Bladder ceremony, the Doll ceremony, and four different types of potlatches, which were shared with the people of neighboring villages. The Animals ceremony included ritual songs and dances, with some participants dressed in special costumes and wearing masks. During the ritual, actors carried out a stage performance of re-enacting hunting and fishing to ensure success at these important food-gathering tasks. The ritual included a masked "clown," who added levity to the event. The Bladder and Doll rituals were intended to pay homage and respect to animal spirits in an effort to learn of future events. Among the potlatch ceremonies, the most serious was the Midwinter Death potlatch. Its purpose "was to honor a dead relative, usually a father, to gain status, and to maintain recip-rocal giving arrangements with other families."[13] Part of the potlatch included the "Hot Dance," which included an entire evening of excessive revelry.

THE KUTCHINS

Another major branch of the Athapaskan peoples of the Alaska-Yukon Territory is the Kutchin (Ku'-chin) or Gwich'in tribe, who have lived in the region of the Peel River Basin to its confluence with the Mackenzie River, as well as the Yukon River region. The name *kutchin* translates as "the People." Among the various bands of the Kutchins are the Hans, Tutchones, and Tananas, whose cultures are similar, and who have been further influenced over the centuries by some Inuit groups, as well as the Tlingits. During the 1700s, when Europeans made their first contact with the Kutchin bands, they may have numbered between 3,000 and 5,000. By 1850, their numbers had dwindled, largely as a result of diseases and epidemics, to around 1,300; by the 1970s, only 700 or so remained.

Ancient Kutchins lived like their Ingalik neighbors, erecting portable, dome-shaped lodges that included curved spruce poles painted red and covered over with caribou hides. These lodges measured approximately 12 to 14 feet long and stood as high as 8 feet. A fire burned inside the lodge for cooking and warmth, and a hole in the top allowed the smoke to escape.

The flooring was made of fir boughs and the outer walls were insulated during the colder months with piles of boughs on the outside, as well as snow. Some Kutchin peoples built their homes of birch bark, and others built semisubterranean homes "of moss blocks covering a wood frame, with gabled roofs."[14]

Their diets consisted of the same foods common to the Ingaliks. They fished during the warmer months of summer, hauling in large catches of pike and whitefish. Along the Yukon River, they caught salmon. They hunted wildlife, including caribou, moose, hare, beaver, and muskrat, with dogs assisting them during their hunts. As with the Ingaliks, the caribou was an important animal, not only for meat, but for the materials it provided to make tools, weapons, and decorative items. The Kutchins also hunted waterfowl.

Kutchin social customs were typical of the tribes in the sub-arctic but with some variations. Tribal members identified themselves through their mothers, not their fathers, because the Kutchins were a matrilineal society. The clan of the mother was the basis of one heritage. Each clan had its own marriage and ceremonial rites. Among the Kutchins, though, the women did not enjoy important status in the day-to-day activities and social structure of clan and village life. It appears that Kutchin women and the elderly were regularly treated with harshness. The women were forced to do much of the domestic work. They "dragged the toboggans, built the shelters, gathered fire-wood, and sometimes ate only after the men were finished."[15] (Despite all these chores for women, the men did the cooking.) Occasionally, Kutchin mothers were known to kill their baby girls in an effort to "spare them from what [their mothers] were enduring."[16] If an elderly person was considered too feeble to move with the tribe, he or she was either killed, often by strangulation, or left behind to die of starvation.

Kutchin clothing styles included shirts and pants, such as a caribou skin shirt that was short waisted, with long tails in front and behind. Some Kutchin women wore oversized shirts so they could carry their babies on their backs and keep them warm. Adornment was common, and the men wore headbands, necklaces, and nose jewelry made of dentalium. The men also painted their faces and used feathers in their hair. Kutchin women often tattooed their chins in the style of Inuit women.

These subarctic people were as superstitious in their religious practices as their neighbors. The remoteness and bleak, wintry world that often surrounded them caused the Kutchins to be "particularly susceptible to fear and awe of the supernatural."[17] As an animistic people, they believed in the embodiment of a spirit in everything, alive or inanimate. Many of these spirits were considered evil or at least mischievous. The people believed that such spirits lurked in the many lakes dotting Kutchin villages, and they believed in the existence of monsters and giants. There were ghosts and demons waiting in the forests and in the rivers, such as the Yukon. These spirits even traveled about on the winds, unseen, ready to do harm to hapless human victims.

The Kutchin people maintained a dreaded fear of the spirit world. In an effort to appease malevolent spirits, the people offered special beads as gifts. To appeal to the spirits before a hunting expedition, Kutchin men prayed to moon-related deities and often burned caribou fat in a fire to ensure success in the hunt. The caribou spirit was special to the Kutchin people, as was the spirit of the bear. Many believed that the caribou and human heart were one and the same, creating a special physical connection between humans and the large, subarctic animal. Other spirits, especially those of animals and birds, were considered good and helpful to humans. The Kutchins, as did other subarctic peoples, tried to make direct contact with such spirits in search of a blessing, such as a skill or quality each animal might be known to possess.

There were special Kutchin ceremonies that recognized the moon and its cycles; important life events, such as puberty and marriage, as well as death; and the wealthy offered potlatches. Such feasts typically included eating, singing, and dancing.

Special holy men, called shamans or medicine men, practiced rituals designed to give people access to animal spirits. Shamans were recognized for their supernatural powers, which they received through fasting and powerful dreams. Often, such spirits were believed to visit humans during their sleep—in dreams. Sometimes, Kutchins sought visions to receive good spirits. The shamans also practiced other supernatural skills. They were believed to have the power to predict the future, heal sickness, and even control natural events, such as the weather.

THE INUITS

The Inuits (many today still refer to these Native Americans as Eskimos), once they arrived in the New World, settled in two primary regions of Alaska. Some established themselves in the Arctic, far to the north. Others ventured across the Bering Land Bridge, hugging the coastlands, and moved southward until they reached the mouth of the Yukon River. Over time, they migrated up the river, perhaps as far as 400 miles from the coast. For thousands of years, the Inuit way of life in the region of the Yukon remained constant, changing little from one generation to the next.

As a people, the Inuits were and remain short in stature, with brownish skin and coarse black hair. They lived in small, multi-family units, with perhaps as many as eight or ten families in the same village. Only rarely would an Inuit village be home to more than 200 people. Each family was considered the core part of Inuit society, but more than one family might often live under the same roof.

For thousands of years, the Inuits have lived in sodden igloos, fashioned out of a "framework of whalebones and driftwood," [18] with squares of sod used to seal over the sides and roof. Like other residents along the Yukon River, including the Athapaskans, the Inuits built their homes around a pit, which made these snug houses semisubterranean. These sod igloos featured only one room and could be entered through a timber-framed sod tunnel along one side. This access tunnel was also used to store frozen meat and whale blubber, serving as a crawl-through "refrigerator." Firewood could also be stored in the tunnel to keep it dry and out of the way of the living space inside the igloo. Inside such snugly built homes, the Inuits did not need to build a fire for warmth because the "interior was warm enough so the smallest children could tumble naked on the robes, and the grownups shed their fur-lined parkas." [19] A small fire might be used for cooking, with the smoke escaping through a smoke hole in the roof. During rain or snowstorms, the smoke hole might be covered over with seal gut. The gut was partially translucent, allowing some light into the sod igloo. Another building could be found in an Inuit village that was the center of life for the residents: The *kashim* was a community gathering house, where tribal members met and socialized and engaged in dances, songs, games, and even religious ceremonies.

The diet of the Inuits along the Yukon consisted of fish and seal and walrus meat harvested during coastal hunting expeditions. Plants and roots supplemented their meals, which were not regularly scheduled, as are breakfast, lunch, and supper today. The Inuits ate whenever they were hungry—the father might tear off pieces of meat from an animal bone or cut off slabs of blubber and hand them to family members. The mother would chew the meat first to soften it up before giving it to younger children. As with other Yukon region tribes, the Inuits ate a snow and berry mixture for dessert. With a minimum of sweets and a diet consisting almost entirely of protein, the Inuits had good, healthy teeth. With so much blubber in their regular diets, these people were often round and a bit plump, but the food fat helped them maintain a healthy body temperature in a harsh winter environment.

To bring in the food needed for their families, Inuit men spent many days hunting and trapping. They used spears and bone fishhooks, as well as nets fashioned from animal sinew. Seal was a common quarry for Inuit hunters. Hunting even took place during the winter months. A hunting party might search along icy beaches for seal or look for them on inlet waters that were frozen over. The hunters looked for a seal's "breathing hole" in an iced-over site, and then established themselves at the hole and waited for the seal to emerge. To protect himself from the wind and other elements, the hunter might build a snow block wall near the hole. After waiting, sometimes for hours, the hunter's time and effort were rewarded when a seal emerged from the opening, and the hunter would jab his spear into his quarry. Once he had the seal up on the ice shelf, he would kill it and return home with food for his family. With so much meat and blubber available at one time, the hunter's family might gorge themselves. This would allow them to go for several days without eating another large meal.

Sometimes, Inuit hunters did not venture out onto frozen water near or on the Alaskan coastline but headed inland, where they looked for bear, moose, and caribou. Because such hunting trips might last for days, the Inuit hunters erected temporary shelters fashioned out of blocks of ice and snow. Along deep snowfields, a hunting party might be able to catch an animal in the snow, trapped and unable to run to safety. If a hunting party were fortunate enough to spear a moose or caribou, it meant hundreds of pounds of meat for their village. Just a single moose, dressed out and skinned, could produce 1,000 pounds of food. During such hunts, the Inuits relied heavily on their dogs to help transport the meat back to their igloos and eventually to their villages.

Inuit men used spears and lances like these to kill such animals as seals, bear, moose, and caribou.

Once the sea ice receded and it was relatively safe to go out in small boats, Inuits situated along the mouth of the Yukon River participated in annual spring whale hunts. A typical Inuit whaling boat measured 40 feet long and consisted of animal skins stretched over a wooden framework or even a whalebone. Such a hunting craft was called an *oomiak*. The most skilled sailor sat in the boat's bow, wielding the harpoon. Taking such a craft out to sea in search of whales was a difficult and dangerous business. If a whale was spotted, the Inuit whalers approached cautiously, with the harpooner lunging his bone-tipped spear into the head of the great beast. A harpooned whale could easily cause a boat to capsize or could smash the boat by charging. If the Inuits managed to kill a whale, they returned to their village, where everyone would eat their fill of whale blubber. Then, they set about skinning the whale, stripping off the "skin, flesh, bone, teeth, flukes, tail, gut, and blood."[20] One such kill would feed a village for many days.

Although whale blubber was considered a sweet delicacy to the Inuits, they also centered their diet on salmon, which they caught when these rich-tasting fish were crowding up the Yukon and other Alaskan rivers by the hundreds of thousands during their spring spawning runs. Salmon was a mainstay of the Inuit diet, and a large amount of the fish was "split from head to tail, cleaned, and stretched to sun dry on big racks"[21] to provide food for the following winter. To round out their diets, Inuit women and children gathered berries, roots, and tundra greens, the Inuits' vegetable alternative. Some of these foods were stored in seal oil in a hole in the ground for winter consumption.

The workhorse for the Inuits was their dog, the Eskimo malamute. These dogs are the descendants of two separate breeds introduced into the Yukon region of eastern Alaska by the Hudson's Bay Company's traders and trappers. Originally, malamutes and huskies were different types of dogs but, over the past two centuries, they have interbred so often that it is difficult today to find a purebred malamute. These strong-shouldered dogs pulled Inuit sleds, with a team comprising between five and nine animals. A well-trained and disciplined malamute dog team can pull a "two-hundred-pound sled twenty-five miles a day."[22]

The Inuits practiced their own style of spiritual rituals and held various religious beliefs. Everything, whether animate or inanimate, had a spirit or *Yua*. Inuit oral tradition and ancient stories told of early times when animals had the ability to become humans. In one such story, "Adventures of a Young Girl," it was told that:

> After a while she saw a fierce old wolf coming over the rise on the bank of the lake. His red tongue hung out. When he came down he went over to the girl and prodded her on her side with his nose. Then he stood up beside her and was transformed into a big husky man in his prime. He wore nothing but a cape of wolfskin.[23]

Inuit spirit traditions explain how animals eventually lost the ability to transform into human form or speak with a human voice. Still, Inuit hunters and others continued to believe they had seen a "human face in the eye of an animal he was pursuing and knew that he had seen its *yua*."[24] Following such an interactive experience, the Inuits might carve a special mask portraying an animal with the human qualities he had witnessed. During the next important festival event, that hunter could tell of his encounter through song while dancing with his mask.

Many Inuits believed in the existence of two different worlds, one visible and one invisible. These two worlds "occupied the same physical space although the spirits of the latter were seldom visible to the occupants of the former."[25] The line separating the two worlds was variable and during singular events in one's life—including birth, the onset of puberty, and death—the line became almost nonexistent, with no barrier between the two. During these times, it was important for each person involved to participate in the correct ritual or ceremony, or the *Tunghat*—the evil spirits—could directly influence one's life, causing mischief or harm.

Inuit holy men, or shamans, were important individuals in the Inuit tribe, providing various services that brought the spirit world together with the physical. Shamans were considered to be healers; able to alter one's physical, psychological, and spiritual conditions. Shamans were also responsible for the annual festivals celebrated by the Inuits. Four such festival events took place each year, including the Asking Festival, the Feast of the Dead, the Bladder Festival, and the Inviting-in Festival. The Asking Festival took place between interrelated villages to reinforce kin relationships and included important gift exchanges. The Feast of the Dead centered on a tribe's desire to provide food, drink, and clothing for loved ones in the next life. During the Bladder Festival, the bladders of all the seals killed by a village were "inflated, painted and hung in the qasgiq,"[26] which is a communal house. Inuits believed that the spirits of seals lived inside their bladders. Following special rituals, dances, and songs, the inflated bladders were taken to the local river or coast and offered to the water. Those seals that had been treated honorably by the Inuit hunters were released and would allow themselves to be killed again during the next seal hunting season. The Inviting-in Festival was held when food was scarce. The Inuit people invited the spirits into their midst to partake of whatever food the village had available. The point was to remind the spirits of animals, birds, fish, and other creatures how important they were in providing food for the tribe during a hunt. Hopefully, the spirits would cooperate and bless the next hunting foray carried out by the Inuit men.

3

Trade Rivals
along the Yukon

For thousands of years, Native Americans, the descendants of Asiatic migrants from the Old World, called the Yukon River and the region of subarctic Alaska home. Although these tribal groups numbered in the dozens and had slightly different cultural lifestyles, their world revolved around hunting, fishing, and living in small familial villages. Their various worlds were more similar than different; their cultures mirrored and reflected one another. By the eighteenth century, however, the world of the Inuits and Athapaskans along the Yukon River and across the Alaskan landscape was about to change dramatically, with a late arrival to their world—the Europeans. The year of first contact was 1741.

That summer, a pair of sailing ships set out to the east from Siberia on an expedition sanctioned by the Russian government. One of the ships, the *St. Peter*, was captained by a 60-year-old Danish sea captain, a veteran explorer named Vitus Bering. Bering had served in the navy of the Russian czars since he was 23 years old. The Danish captain was soon sailing through waters he had navigated in 1728—a strait between the easternmost point of Siberia and the western coast of modern-day Alaska. During that earlier voyage, Bering had become convinced that the strait, which today bears his name, was a watery chasm dividing the continents of Asia and North America. On that earlier voyage, though, the Danish captain had not actually reached the shores of Alaska; he had failed to spot land because of a heavy fog. The 1741 voyage represented Bering's attempt to prove his theory. (For additional information on this Danish sea captain, enter "Vitus Bering" into any search engine and browse the many sites listed.)

Despite Bering's skill and experience at sea, his 1741 voyage did not go well. His two ships became separated during stormy weather and permanently lost contact with one another. By July, however, they each reached the coast of Alaska, with Bering's ship landing just east of Prince William Sound. Already, the

In 1741, while sailing under the employ of the Russian government, Danish captain Vitus Jonassen Bering became the first European to discover the Alaska coast. Unfortunately, Bering never made it back to Russia—his ship, the *St. Peter*, ran aground on what is today Bering Island. Bering, along with 19 members of his crew, perished.

crew of the *St. Peter* was becoming ill, many with scurvy, which was caused by a vitamin deficiency. Bering himself contracted the disease. After exploring further, Bering decided not to remain in his newly discovered lands but instead was determined to return to Siberia. His ship never made it back to Russia. Heavy seas threw the *St. Peter* onto coastal rocks along Bering Island.

Stranded, 20 men on board the Russian sailing ship died by December, including Vitus Bering. Those who remained alive survived by eating fish and seal meat. They constructed a 40-foot boat from the wreckage of the *St. Peter* and, the following spring, finally reached the same Siberian harbor from which they had sailed the previous year. Bering's second ship had returned to its home harbor the previous October.

Although the 1741 voyage of Vitus Bering appeared to end in abject failure, his discovery of the Alaskan coast would prove of great importance to the Russian government. Based on his claim and discovery, the Russians followed up Bering's voyage by dispatching fur trappers and traders. Bering's crew, in fact, had returned to Russia with 800 sea otter skins, "more prized even than sable on Chinese markets because of their plush density." [27] Russian fur traders, known as *promyshlenniki,* began extending their fur hunting, trapping, and trading grounds farther east with each passing year. By the 1790s, the Russian fur trade was among the most lucrative in the world. The sea otter became so valued that a single otter fur might sell for three times more than an average European worker's annual wage. The profits from the trade lured ever-increasing numbers of intrepid fortune seekers and fur men.

After nine decades of exploring and exploiting the Aleutian Islands for furs, the Russians had finally advanced so far along the Alaskan coast that, by 1829, they reached the mouth of the Yukon River. Four years later, the Russians established a trading post 60 miles up from the Yukon's mouth, on St. Michael Island. In 1834, an intrepid Russian fur trader, Andree Glazanoff, and four companions set out overland to the east with two dogsleds until they reached the head of the Anvik River. In unfamiliar country, the Russians had a difficult time finding food, but, fortunately, they reached an Inuit village, where they were given meals of rotten fish. Pressing on, the party continued down the Anvik River to its confluence with the Yukon, which they reached on January 24, 1834. Glazanoff's arrival at Alaska's great interior river is recognized as one of the important European discoveries of the Yukon.

Soon, the Russians were trading with the Athapaskans in Alaska's interior, along the Yukon and other rivers. At Anvik, Glazanoff met with Inuits in their kashim and traded them tobacco for bear meat and blubber. The local Indians were intrigued by the Russians' metal tools, knives, and a kettle, and they made it clear to Glazanoff that they were willing to trade for such goods, but Glazanoff and his men had not entered the region to trade. They had been sent out to explore along the Yukon and its tributaries to determine the possibilities of trade with the Athapaskans—and they discovered that these possibilities had great potential.

In the years that followed, Russian fur traders proceeded farther and farther up the Yukon and established trade with several Native communities and villages. Agents of the Russian-American Trading Company could be found as far as 500 miles up the Yukon. The trading involved Native Americans along the Yukon bartering furs for a wide variety of trade goods. The practice was new to all the interior tribes, and it changed their way of life dramatically. Prior to the arrival of the Russians, the Athapaskans and Inuits generally hunted only for food and survival. With the Europeans in their midst, they began hunting and trapping furs for an additional reason—trade. The Indians were soon trading furs, animal hides, and dried salmon for such manufactured and exotic goods as iron cooking pots, metal arrowheads, bolts of cloth, metal tools, needles, and beads. Sometimes, the local Indians collected anything discarded by the Europeans, including metal boxes, cartons, and cans, which could be used for storage. Small empty barrels were collected and prized by the Athapaskans as ideal for collecting snow. The age of metal had arrived for the Natives along the Yukon River and its tributaries. Russian traders also supplied these subarctic Natives with such metal goods as steel traps, axes, harpoons, and firearms. The Russians, as they spread farther upriver, established trading outposts to provide permanent sites where Indians could deliver their furs for trading.

THE ESTABLISHMENT OF FORT YUKON

By the 1840s, a century had passed since the arrival of the Danish sea captain Vitus Bering on the shores of Alaska and the establishment of the Russian fur trade in the Alaskan subarctic. In the meantime, the Russians had made their way hundreds of miles up the Yukon River and had established interior trading connections with the Athapaskans. By 1847, though, the Russians were going to face the challenge of another European interloper into the region of the Yukon River. Leading that vanguard was a young Scotsman, an agent of the British-owned Hudson's Bay Company, which had been trapping and trading furs in eastern Canada for more than two centuries.

Alexander Hunter Murray was a tall, handsome Scot, who entered the Yukon wilderness as a seasoned veteran of the fur-trading business. He had worked for many years for the American Fur Company and was widely known in the American fur trade as the director of the post at Fort Union, located at the confluence of the Yellowstone and Missouri Rivers on the border between modern-day North Dakota and Montana. By 1847, he joined the Hudson's Bay Company to seek further adventure. That year, he was dispatched to the Yukon Territory with orders to establish a trading post at the confluence of the Porcupine River—a western river that flowed from Canada to Alaska—and the Yukon River. If Murray succeeded, the Hudson's Bay Company would have an outlet to the Pacific Ocean. It did not matter to the company or to Murray that his movements into Alaska would place him in Russian territory, with no rights to build such a fort.

Setting out from the Hudson's Bay Company's outpost of Fort McPherson in northern Yukon Territory, Murray was accompanied by another Scotsman, a carpenter named McKenzie, and eight others, including French-Canadians; some of whom were part Indian, including one who served as the expedition's interpreter. Carrying 40-pound packs on their backs, the Murray party trekked through hundreds of miles of subarctic wilderness, following rivers and traversing the Yukon wilderness. In his journal, Murray noted: "We waded most of the way knee deep, and often to the middle of sludge and water. The mosquitoes had already begun their ravages."[28] Three days out from Fort McPherson, Murray and his men reached La Pierre's House, another trading post. There, Murray was given a crude bark boat, a "combination canoe and barge, about thirty feet long, with the stern covered with birch bark."[29] The men loaded their supplies and equipment onboard the boat, which Murray would call the *Pioneer*. It would soon become the first boat made by non-Indians to reach the waters of the Upper Yukon River.

For days, the Murray party pushed downstream on the Bell River, then known as the Porcupine. He traded with Indians along the way and encouraged them to bring their furs down-river to the post he intended to build. Along the Porcupine River, the swift current sped the *Pioneer* on. Murray created a map of the river, using a compass. As he and his men traveled through the rough Yukon wilderness, they scouted for possible trading post sites. Here and there, local Indians showed Murray gold flakes and dust that sprinkled the river gravels, but the Scotsman was uninterested. He and his company were after another form of treasure—furs.

After eight days of travel, covering 450 miles downriver from La Pierre's House, Murray's raft reached the waters of the Yukon River. Advised by local Indians of a good location for a post, Murray and his men traveled three miles up the Yukon to a promising site, a high-ground location that overlooked the river. The Athapaskans in the area were already informing one another of the arrival of the Europeans up and down the Yukon as Murray and his men unloaded their raft and prepared an encampment. One of the Indians Murray spoke with told him that he had traded with the Russians downstream and that they were planning to move upriver. Murray and his men remained watchful in case they encountered a Russian party. Writing in his journal, Murray noted: "I . . . determined to keep a sharp lookout in case of surprise. Mr. McKenzie and I divided the night watch between us, a rule laid down and strictly adhered to when Indians were with us."[30]

The following morning, Murray and his men were awakened at 4 A.M. by musket shots. The Hudson's Bay Company men took their own guns in hand, fearing the Russians were about to attack. Instead, at the edge of the Yukon, they saw nearly two dozen Indian canoes approach, loaded with furs, fresh meat, and dried fish. Soon, both parties were sitting along the river, engaging in a special Indian ceremony, which included singing, dancing, and smoking special pipes. Murray explained how he and his men were different white men than the Russians: They would trade more fairly with the Indians, and they intended to erect a trading post so they could trade with the local Athapaskans year-round, rather than once annually, as the Russians did. More ceremonies followed, and a feast, which lasted through the next night. The Indians appeared prepared to accept the presence of their new trading partners.

The following day, despite a lack of sleep, Murray and his partners began building the trading post that they had promised the Indians the previous day. The log post would measure 24 feet in length by 14 feet. In less than one week, the makeshift post was ready for occupation and Murray set up business, but the fortress wall still had to be raised. Soon, the work on the fort was under way, with the logs hauled in on the

Pioneer from islands along the Yukon River. At the same time, the Indians were showing up in significant numbers, with furs in hand, ready to trade. Even before the fort was completed, Murray was doing a brisk business trading blankets, axes, knives, files and rasps, powder horns, and an endless number of beads, which the Natives prized, for furs, deerskins, and sinew.

Before long, the Indians were asking the Hudson's Bay Company men to sell them guns, but Murray refused. When a pair of Indian warriors sneaked into the post and tried to steal some muskets, Murray pulled his flintlock pistol and relieved them of their stolen goods, while informing them: "Tell them if anyone sets foot in the store again, I will shoot him dead."[31] It was the last time Murray faced that sort of challenge.

By the end of August, the fort was nearly completed and measured 46 feet long and 26 feet wide. Inside the log building, the Hudson's Bay Company men lived in five interconnected rooms, where they cooked, ate, worked, slept, kept the company's records, and traded with the Indians. The walls provided significant protection from possible raids, whether at the hands of the local Natives or the Russians from downstream. The walls "were bulletproof and contained small loopholes neatly fitted with blocks of wood. These plugs could be removed in case of an attack, and a gun barrel inserted in each."[32]

During the months that followed, the men added to their frontier facilities, building a boathouse, a smokehouse where fish could be dried, and scaffolds where meat was stored high above the ground, away from bears and other predators. The trade at the fort was brisk but, with each passing month, Murray's supply of trade goods was dwindling. He sent five of his men with two dogsleds back to La Pierre's House for more trade items, but when they returned, they brought back much less than the fort needed to continue trading with the Indians. Murray noted in his diary: "Without beads, and plenty of them, you can do little or no good here."[33]

(continued on page 42)

THE UNITED STATES PURCHASES ALASKA FROM THE RUSSIANS

For nearly a century, the Russian fur trappers and traders harvested thousands of sea otters from Alaskan waters annually. By the 1820s, though, sea otters were on the verge of extinction, and those Russians who continued to make the sea voyage into subarctic waters in search of furs found too few of them to make a profit. By that time, otters were even becoming scarce as far south as Oregon and California. The era of Russian fur extraction from Alaska was coming to an end.

During their quest for furs, the Russians had colonized Alaska. They had established trading centers and towns along the coast, and had built government buildings and Russian Orthodox churches, with their distinct onion domes. The Russian capital in Alaska, Sitka, on the coast of Baranov Island, south of Glacier Bay, had served as the seat of government, and from there Russian governors tenuously ruled over a fur empire. Sitka was 3,000 miles from the nearest sizeable Russian port and the cost of shipping supplies to the remote Russian villages in Alaska was high—$330 a ton from Siberia.

By the 1850s, the czarist government in St. Petersburg was prepared to abandon its expensive colonial attempts in Alaska due to the debt it had accrued in fighting the Crimean War (1854–1856). The United States, whose star was certainly on the rise in western North America, including the Pacific Northwest, was the most likely candidate. The United States had already made California the thirty-first state in the union, removed the Spanish-Mexican presence along the northern Pacific coast with the defeat of Mexico through war in the late 1840s, and negotiated control of the Oregon Country from Russia's longtime fur rival in Alaska, Great Britain. Alaska's future appeared to lie with the United States.

The outbreak of the American Civil War stalled any negotiations concerning the United States' purchase of Alaska from the Russians. By 1866, however, Czar Alexander II sent instructions to Russia's ambassador in Washington, D.C., Baron Edouard de Stoeckl, to open talks with U.S. Secretary of State William H. Seward, who had favored Alaska's annexation for years. The Russians were in the mood to divest themselves of Alaska and their asking price was low, $7.2 million—equivalent to about two cents per acre. Whereas Seward believed he had negotiated a bargain, he was not aware that Czar Alexander had informed Stoeckl he was willing to accept an offer as low as $5 million. The U.S. Senate ratified the treaty quickly, on April 4, 1867. (To grease the wheels of Congress, Stoeckl had offered generous bribes to several key senators for their support.)

Sitka, Alaska, shown here in 1892, was the headquarters of the Russian-American Company and the center of the Russian fur trade. By the 1850s, with fur-bearing animals such as seals becoming scarce, Russia abandoned its fur-trade operations in the area and sold what later became the state of Alaska to the United States in 1867.

Despite the apparent real estate coup negotiated by Seward, some Americans did not support the purchase, considering Alaska to be nothing but a frozen, remote wasteland. Newspaper editorials mocked the secretary of state, calling his purchase "Seward's Folly," and Alaska "Seward's icebox" and "Walrussia." U.S. troops arrived in Sitka by October, however, and relieved Russian forces as the Russia governor turned Alaska over to the United States.

The Russians had tapped the fur market and made great profits for decades on their efforts. They left Alaska believing that they had left little behind of any value. In doing so, they abandoned the great untapped riches of a land whose interior they had never explored, where, within a generation, gold would be discovered along the Yukon River and its tributaries, creating another lucrative era of exploitation in Alaskan history.

(continued from page 39)

Over that first winter, Murray and his men remained in Fort Yukon, surviving on the local wildlife, as well as wild cranberries. The men had planted a garden the previous fall, but the late season had only produced a bushel of potatoes of varying sizes, mostly small, which Murray decided to keep as seed potatoes for the next summer. By the spring of 1848, Murray, still needing trade goods, sent a letter to Hudson's Bay headquarters in central Canada: "Guns and beads, beads and guns is all the cry in our country. Please to excuse me for repeating this so often, but I cannot be too importunate. The rise or fall of our establishment on the Youcon [sic] depends principally on the supply of these articles."[34] When no supplies arrived, Murray and his men built a pair of 38-foot-long trade boats, a common size used by Canadian traders, and set out for La Pierre's House, leaving McKenzie in command of the fort. After a grueling four months, Murray finally returned to his remote outpost, with a large supply of trade goods, as well as a woman he introduced as his new wife. With the shelves of his post restocked with all the items sought by Indians who appeared with furs for trade, Murray and his men were soon engaged in more business than ever.

Within a few months, the party of intrepid Hudson's Bay Company employees marked their first year in the wilderness along the banks of the Yukon River. It was to be the beginning of many years of successful trading for Murray on behalf of the company. Murray would command Fort Yukon until 1856, when he was promoted to chief trader and transferred to other Hudson's Bay Company fort-posts back east. Murray did not completely retire from wilderness trading until 1867—the year the United States purchased Alaska from the Russians. Two years later, Murray's fort was reached by the Americans, who informed the Hudson's Bay Company men that their fort was in Alaska, not the Yukon Territory, and forced them to surrender the trading post to them.

4

The Explorations
of Robert Campbell

The Russians had reached the Lower Yukon and established trade along it as early as the 1830s, and the British, through Alexander Murray, had arrived on the middle part of the Yukon by the late 1840s. The upper reaches of Alaska's greatest river still remained a region unexplored and untapped by Europeans but, on the heels of Murray's efforts, another Hudson's Bay Company trading agent was preparing to establish his company's presence on the Upper Yukon. Like Murray, he was a Scotsman—Robert Campbell.

In the spring of 1836, the Hudson's Bay Company operated a post, Fort Simpson, at the confluence of the Mackenzie and Liard Rivers, in the midst of "some of the most difficult, mountain-tangled wilderness in North America."[35] Campbell arrived at the fort that spring just in time to witness the arrival of a Hudson's Bay Company clerk who had recently been dispatched to establish a distant post at Dease Lake. The frightened clerk told his fellow traders that he had encountered local Indians who warned him and his men that a war party of hundreds of Chilkoot Indians, a subdivision of the Tlingits, was headed his way to challenge the presence of the Hudson's Bay Company and their trade with interior tribes. The Chilkoots were partners with the Russians far downriver and had come to control the trade between them and the upriver tribes. The Hudson's Bay Company men were considered challengers to the trading power of the Chilkoots. In a panic from the news, the clerk admitted that he and his men had not only abandoned their march to Dease Lake, but they had left "their outfit of trade goods for the new post scattered along the trail."[36]

The newly arrived Campbell was outraged at the panicky response of the Hudson's Bay Company clerk and volunteered to establish the post at Dease Lake himself. After some difficulty raising an expedition of recruits, he finally set out, but it was nearly winter, and he and his party managed only to reach Fort Halkett, a remote, underdefended Hudson's Bay Company

The Chilkoot Indians served as trade intermediaries between the Russians and other Indian tribes who lived farther up the Yukon River. Though agents of Great Britain's Hudson's Bay Company made repeated attempts to trade with the Chilkoots, the tribe remained hostile toward them and instead favored trade with the Russians.

outpost. Leaving his trade goods at the fort, Campbell continued on toward Dease Lake. He finally reached the point in the wilderness of southwestern Yukon Territory where the frightened clerk had abandoned his trade goods on the trail. Although the foodstuffs had been eaten by wildlife in the area, the remainder of the goods was still tied up in large bundles, undisturbed. With no sign of the Chilkoots in the vicinity, Campbell and his men packed up the abandoned trade items and hauled them to Fort Halkett, where they remained through the winter.

The following spring, Campbell and his men set out for Dease Lake with their vast supply of trade items. They reached Dease Lake and, by July, had erected a small trading post.

While much of the construction went on, Campbell, along with a pair of Indians and an interpreter, took time to explore the largely unknown region. After just two days out, Campbell and his party reached the Tuya River, where they found a rickety, pine pole bridge spanning the waterway. On the opposite bank, they found an abandoned Indian hut. An iron pot inside the hut revealed to Campbell that these local Indians had already established trade contacts with the Russians downriver.

Campbell and his men remained in the lodge overnight. The following morning, a group of Indians appeared at the hut, and identified themselves as Nehannis Indians. Campbell conversed with them, attempting to convince the Natives to trade with the Hudson's Bay Company men, but the Nehannis were intimidated by the Chilkoots, who lived just 12 miles downriver. Although the Nehannis chief refused at first, Campbell convinced him to lead him to the Chilkoot camp. When Campbell reached the Indian campsite, he realized he had stumbled into the annual meeting between the Chilkoots and a wide cross section of Native tribes, who had arrived from hundreds of miles away. Because the Chilkoots traded as middlemen for the Russians, the presence of Campbell as a representative for the rival Hudson's Bay Company might have caused the Chilkoots to turn on him and his men. Unafraid, Campbell approached the Chilkoots well armed, carrying a "[knife] and two pistols in his belt, and a double-barreled percussion gun." [37] As Campbell walked into the encampment, many Indians made hostile gestures, but the intrepid Scot fired one of his handguns to frighten the warriors who were challenging him. The Chilkoots' chief asked Campbell and his men to enter his lodge and soon the two men were engaged in serious trade talks. Despite every reassurance made by Campbell, though, the chief remained unconvinced that the Hudson's Bay Company would be better trade partners for the Chilkoots. The chief allowed Campbell and his men to leave unharmed, but Campbell was undeterred, despite the chief having made no commitment to his offers.

In direct defiance, Campbell moved to high ground within sight of the Chilkoot encampment and placed a Hudson's Bay Company flag on a tree limb, in effect announcing that he was in business as a local trader. Soon, Campbell received a direct warning from a female member of the Nehannis tribe that he and his men were going to be attacked by the Chilkoots and their Indian allies. Campbell shrewdly evacuated his position, and he and his men marched all night back to the new post at Dease Lake. Campbell then had to make an important decision, whether to remain in his new post and risk an attack by the Chilkoots or one of their allied tribes, or abandon his post and return to safety back east. Campbell stubbornly decided to remain at Dease Lake. Throughout the following winter, the fort came under attack several times by small bands of Indian warriors, but the Hudson's Bay Company men held their post. For safety's sake, the men were forced to remain inside the post, unable to go out and hunt or gather firewood. After many weeks, the post's food supply was seriously depleted and Campbell and his men were forced to eat anything they could, including the "parchment covering the window openings."[38] Only a new supply of food provided by the Nehannis managed to keep the men alive but only for the moment.

As the winter dragged on, Campbell's men began to suffer dramatically, growing weak from hunger. One of his men died. Indian attacks came repeatedly, and only the superior marksmanship of the Hudson's Bay Company men kept the invaders outside the post. By May, the post was nearly starved out, the men "boiling the last of the parchment and the netting on their snowshoes, [gulping] down the nauseating mess."[39] Desperate, Campbell ordered the post's evacuation, and he and his men set out through hostile territory until they stumbled into the safety of Fort Hackett. Fortunately, they all managed to make it back alive.

Once Campbell recovered from the Dease Lake ordeal, he reported back to company headquarters at Fort Simpson. There, he received new orders from the company's governor, George Simpson, to return to the Yukon wilderness and explore other portions of the region. By May 1840, he was on his way, leaving by canoe with three Indians and his loyal interpreter.

Campbell's exploring took him from Fort Simpson, located at the confluence of the Liard and Mackenzie Rivers, down the Liard to an interior body of water he called Frances Lake. From there, he crossed into the valley of the Pelly River, a major tributary of the Yukon, which he named for an official of the Hudson's Bay Company. To mark his having reached the Pelly, Campbell nailed a company flag to a tree and carved his initials and the date on it. Then, the fearless Scot returned to Fort Hackett and remained there for yet another difficult winter in the Yukon wilderness.

THE ESTABLISHMENT OF FORT SELKIRK

Campbell's exploring in the Yukon region was not yet over. From 1841 through 1842, Campbell further developed the Hudson's Bay Company trade out of Fort Hackett and established the post at Frances Lake. Then, in the early summer of 1843, he and six companions returned to the Pelly River. Once they had constructed a pair of canoes, the seven-man team began a watery trip down the Pelly, until they reached a major confluence a week later. As they passed into the mouth of a new river, Campbell named it Lewes River, after the chief trader at Fort Simpson. Although the intrepid Scot had no way of knowing it at the time, the Lewes was in fact the headwaters of the Yukon River. Soon, he and his men met with a new Indian tribe, the Stick, or Yukon, Indians, who had never seen a white man. Meeting with the Yukon chief, Campbell was informed that warlike tribes lived downriver, including some who practiced cannibalism. With his men fearful from the news, Campbell

Four Yukon Natives stand outside of Fort Selkirk. The Hudson's Bay Company fort, located at the confluence of the Pelly and Upper Yukon Rivers, was burned down by Chilkoot Indians during the summer of 1852 and was not reestablished as a trading post by the Hudson's Bay Company until 1938.

was forced to abandon his advance down the Lewes River. He and his comrades arrived at the Hudson's Bay Company post at Frances Lake and remained there through yet another winter.

Over the following years, Campbell continued his endless explorations on behalf of the Hudson's Bay Company. In 1846, he established yet another post, this time on the Pelly River, where he remained for two years. By 1848, he and about a dozen men built another trading post at the confluence of the Pelly and Lewes Rivers, called Fort Selkirk, the first trading post built on the upper end of the Yukon River. Here, Campbell remained for another three years, working to consolidate the trade connections in the region of Fort Selkirk with neighboring tribes. He remained restless, though, wanting to explore the

(continued on page 52)

DETERMINING THE SOURCE OF THE YUKON RIVER

Today, the Yukon River is a well-known waterway, thoroughly mapped and studied by many geographers, river experts, geologists, and hydrologists; but for a century, the waters of the Upper Yukon River were in dispute. As more and more exploration was undertaken during the nineteenth century, the river was redefined to its current length. How the modern-day Yukon would finally be delineated on the maps of the twentieth century is a long and involved story of exploration, misunderstandings, tradition, and information gathering.

European fur traders traveled farther and farther into the great Canadian Northwest by various routes, reaching a wide variety of rivers, large and small. Until those rivers were completely explored, they could not be mapped out and mistakes were made. In 1843, the great Scottish explorer and trader for the Hudson's Bay Company, Robert Campbell, believed that the river upstream from the Pelly was a mere tributary and gave it a new name, the Lewes River, after the company's chief benefactor, John Lee Lewes. By 1846, another Hudson's Bay Company explorer, a Scot named John Bell, reached the same stretch of river several hundred miles down-river, and called those waters the Youcon River, after a local Indian name, *Yuchoo*, which translated as "great river." To add to the confusion, this name replaced a previous one used by the Russians a decade earlier, *Kwikhpak*, an Aleut Inuit word also meaning "great river."

Until the 1880s, then, the upper waters of the Yukon River were known as the Lewes River. The river upstream to the Pelly River was considered Bell's Youcon or Yukon. Later, local tradition extended the Yukon to Lake Laberge. Above Lake Laberge, to its headwaters in southwestern Yukon Territory, the river was referred to as the Lewes River. Maps made the distinction between the two interconnected rivers.

Then, in 1883, U.S. Army First Lieutenant Frederick Schwatka, changed the history—and the maps—of the Upper Yukon River. Schwatka, an 1871 graduate of West Point, was an extremely talented officer; one who would eventually become both a lawyer and practicing medical doctor. He was also a natural born explorer, whose military expeditions took him across the Arctic region from Canada to Siberia. In 1883, he was sent north from Washington Territory "in view of the frequent reports of the disturbance of peace between the whites and Indians in Alaska."* Lt. Schwatka was dispatched along with an Army doctor, three enlisted men, and a civilian.

After he and his party had scaled Chilkoot Pass in Yukon Territory, Schwatka reached Lake Lindemann. By mid-July, the military party began building a log raft measuring 15 by 40 feet that included a sail, bow, stern, and side oars. Christened the *Resolute*, the raft was delivered into the waters of the local river, traditionally called the Lewes. For the next 1,300 miles, Schwatka and his men were engaged in a harrowing float down the Lewes and Yukon Rivers, passing over treacherous rapids but managing to keep their frail watercraft intact. As the party advanced through the Yukon region, Schwatka renamed many sites that had been named decades earlier by other non-Indian explorers and fur traders.

One name change he made was that of the Lewes River. Through his observations, Schwatka became convinced that the Lewes River carried much more water into the Yukon River downstream than the Pelly River, which at that time was considered the primary source of the Yukon. Schwatka determined that the Lewes was not actually a tributary of the Pelly River, but was the headwaters of the Yukon River itself. With the stroke of his pen, Schwatka changed the name of the Lewes to the Yukon.

The change, however, was not immediately recognized. Locals saw no reason to alter their view of the Lewes and, 15 years later, the Geographic Board of Canada voted to ignore Lt. Schwatka's renaming and ruled that the Lewes River would remain known by its long-standing name. Despite the ruling of the Geographic Board, other Americans in the Yukon region were already referring to the Lewes as the Yukon. The year was 1898, and the Yukon Valley was besieged by tens of thousands of gold prospectors who only knew the Lewes as the Yukon River.

The Lewes-Yukon controversy continued for the next 50 years, but on May 5, 1949, the Geographic Board of Canada reconsidered the decision made by its nineteenth-century counterparts, and officially renamed the Lewes River as the upper reaches of the Yukon River. The Lewes River would be forever erased from all future maps.

* Morgan B. Sherwood, *Exploration of Alaska, 1865–1900* (New Haven, Conn.: Yale University Press, 1965), 99.

(continued from page 49)

streams he had not yet mastered. By the early summer of 1851, Campbell, long a veteran of the Yukon region, set out downriver from Fort Selkirk on the Lewes.

This exploration of Robert Campbell became one of his most important. As he and a party of Hudson's Bay Company trappers and Natives advanced, the river widened and passed through a region of incredible scenery and abundant wildlife. Along the way, some of the men found bits of gold dust and some nuggets, but Campbell ignored the would-be treasure, believing nothing held greater value in trade than fur. The Indians the party encountered had never seen white men before and still lived as primitively as any Campbell had ever encountered; untouched by European traders. The only evidence the Hudson's Bay Company men saw to indicate that there had been at least some contact with Indians downriver was a few beads the Indians used to decorate their caribou clothing.

As they progressed, Campbell and his men passed the site where the great gold rush town of Dawson would one day stand, reached the confluence of the Yukon and Klondike Rivers, and soon paddled their canoes across the border between Alaska and Yukon Territory. The beautiful scenery began to recede into the distance and the party passed numerous islands as the river widened further. As they approached the junction of the Porcupine and Yukon Rivers, the men saw a familiar sight ahead. It was Fort Yukon, the "red flag of the Hudson's Bay Company"[40] flying from a pole above a scattering of post buildings. Campbell hailed the post, and the traders emerged as excited to see the Campbell party as Campbell and his men were to have arrived at a welcome resting place along the river. The significance of the Hudson's Bay Company expedition was not lost on any of his men. Campbell had become "the first white man to record his journey through the middle Yukon and proving that the Lewes of the Upper Yukon Basin was the same river as the Youcon."[41] His voyage from Fort Selkirk had proven once and for all that Fort Selkirk and Fort Yukon were, indeed, on the same water route.

After a break from the challenges of the river, Campbell and his intrepid party continued their explorations, moving up the Porcupine and Bell Rivers, followed by an overland trek and then passage up the Mackenzie River north to Fort Simpson, regional headquarters of the Hudson's Bay Company. Once he and his men had accumulated a significant supply of trade goods and food provisions for themselves, they set out back south to Fort Yukon and then up the river for the return trip to Fort Selkirk, reaching the fort by October 1851. The return was a satisfying one to Campbell, who was now looking "forward to a prosperous winter's trade in the fort he had built, on the river he had discovered."[42]

Events did not cooperate for Campbell, though. The following summer, Fort Selkirk came under attack by Chilkoots, who had always considered the Hudson's Bay Company outpost as an infringement on their trading status in the region. Campbell himself was attacked outside the post and narrowly escaped with his life. Fortunately, he reached a canoe and, along with a comrade, paddled downriver. In the distance, the two men could see the smoke rising from Fort Selkirk—the Chilkoots had set the post ablaze. When Campbell and his associate returned the next day, they found Fort Selkirk reduced to cinder and ash. There was nothing for Campbell to do but to take a canoe downriver to the relative safety of Fort Yukon. In time, the valiant Scottish trader and explorer made his way back east to the Hudson's Bay Company headquarters, which were now located in Montreal. Campbell requested men from Sir George Simpson for a campaign to return to the Yukon River region and "square up with the Chilkoots,"[43] but Simpson prudently assigned Campbell to another, more important, assignment as director of yet another Hudson's Bay Company trading post. As for Campbell and his years of service spent trading and exploring in the Yukon country, he was never to return to the river basin where he had spent so many productive, exciting, and rewarding years. As for Fort Selkirk, although the post was gone, the settlement lived on at the site and served as a stop for prospectors bound for the Klondike gold rush during the 1890s. As for their trading post, the Hudson's Bay Company did not venture to rebuild the outpost until 1938. (For additional information on Canada's oldest corporation, enter "Hudson's Bay Company" into any search engine and browse the many sites listed.)

5

Gold Rush along the Yukon

Following the U.S. government's purchase of Alaska from the Russians in 1867, the Yukon River region remained for decades a largely untapped, underpopulated piece of subarctic real estate. Much of the economic activity scattered across the vast region still centered on the long-standing fur trade. Within 30 years of the purchase, however, the history of Alaska and that of the Yukon Territory was experiencing extraordinary change in the form of one of the most concentrated, feverish gold rushes in U.S. and Canadian history—the Klondike gold rush of 1896 to 1898. Though this period was the height of the gold rush in the Yukon Valley, gold was first found there in the 1860s, just as the territory of Alaska changed hands from Russia to the United States.

EARLY GOLD SEEKERS ALONG THE YUKON

During the first half of the nineteenth century, the fur traders of such companies as the Russian-American Trading Company and Hudson's Bay Company had discovered gold along the Yukon without fanfare or even prolonged interest. The profits made from fur-trading were so significant that the traces of gold they saw in streambeds or along riverbanks did not lure them away from the lucrative fur-trade. In 1869, however, after the news that gold had been discovered in Alaska reached the ears of seasoned gold prospectors in such places as California, Colorado, and Idaho, the lure of gold drew prospectors north by the thousands. The vast majority of these newly arrived treasure hunters concentrated their gold-seeking efforts along the southern coastline of Alaska and the larger islands off the coast. Gold was discovered in 1871 near Sitka, and a boom town, Silver Bay, was established, but that strike "petered out several years later, and these mines were deserted."[44] Many prospectors were disappointed in the amounts of gold they discovered, and nearly as many as those who had entered Alaska and Yukon Territory in search of the precious metal left the frozen country within a few years, disappointed and broke.

Although most early prospectors concentrated their efforts along the Alaskan coast, by the early 1870s two parties of gold seekers had moved into the interior of British Columbia and had begun searching for gold north of the Yukon River. Two of these intrepid prospectors—Leroy Napoleon "Jack" McQuesten and Arthur Harper—would find exactly what they were looking for. As for McQuesten, a New England native, seeking gold was a way of life. He had traveled to California during the 1849 gold rush and then pushed north a decade later in Canada, prospecting along the Fraser River. Harper was an Irish immigrant who had also been enticed at an early age to seek gold in the American West. When Harper and McQuesten arrived in the Yukon River region in 1873, they entered a world nearly uninhabited by white men. Those whites in the Yukon region numbered fewer than a dozen and nearly all of them were involved in the fur trade.

After arriving in the interior in 1873, McQuesten became an employee of the Alaska Commercial Company to provide himself a regular income while he prospected for gold on the side. The following year, he opened a trading post, Fort Reliance, on the Yukon River. Arthur Harper soon became one of McQuesten's partners in the fur-trading business. While McQuesten ran the post, his employees, including Harper, searched for gold when they were not directly involved in fur trading. These men discovered gold, but in small quantities, with none of them making any significant strikes. With each passing year, as more and more would-be gold seekers reached the Yukon region, strikes took place with greater frequency. In 1878, a prospector named George Holt tramped to the headwaters of the Yukon River, where he received two gold nuggets in a trade with a local Indian and heard stories of greater gold prospects along the great northern river. Gold was discovered in 1880 along the Hootalinqua River but in limited amounts. A limited strike was made the following year along the Lewes stretch of the Upper Yukon. In 1882, a dozen prospectors showed up together at Fort Reliance, with "gold enough in their moose-hide pokes to pay for their purchases."[45] They informed McQuesten that at least 100 miners were searching for gold along the Upper Yukon.

With each passing year, the dogged perseverance of these few gold seekers began to pay off. As for McQuesten and Harper, they remained dedicated to remaining in the region, continuing to profit by the increase in trade brought on by the arrival of ever-increasing numbers of miners. By 1883, they joined together in a new partnership, along with a third associate, Alfred Mayo, and formed their own trading firm with the backing of the Alaska Commercial Company. Mayo was a "onetime circus acrobat driven north by wanderlust, given to practical jokes and blessed with a dry wit."[46] Three years later, they were in business at the mouth of the Stewart River, where significant strikes were soon discovered. For McQuesten, Harper, and Mayo, the move to the Stewart proved fortuitous.

During the summer of 1884, one group of prospectors spent a season searching for gold and managed to discover a productive pocket on the upper river, with the worth of the gold amounting to $100,000. Such strikes, though, did not result in a general stampede of gold seekers to the Yukon region. They continued to filter into British Columbia in small groups of two or three, fanning out along the various tributaries of the main river. In the meantime, such posts as Fort Reliance were doing a brisk business, not only trading furs with the local Native Americans, but providing supplies to the prospectors who passed through. As for Harper, he and a group of associates panned along the Stewart. Other prospectors reached the same river and moved farther up its banks, searching for metal. One group "prospected the bars of the river, thawing them with fire in order to free the gravels."[47] That year, dozens of miners swarmed up and down the Stewart, and their efforts produced more than $80,000 worth of gold.

All these strikes, however, were soon dwarfed by what took place during the 1886 season as miners hit it big along the river known as Fortymile. That year, approximately 200 miners entered the Yukon region from Skagway, having crossed over the daunting Chilkoot Pass. Most of them spent the prospecting season panning the Stewart River. Collectively, they panned out $100,000 worth of "fine placer gold."[48]

This led McQuesten and his associates to erect a trading post at the mouth of the Stewart, and McQuesten traveled to San Francisco to order more supplies. During the winter of 1886–1887, Harper, who was working the trading post in McQuesten's absence, hired a pair of volunteers to send word to McQuesten. The two men barely reached Dyea Inlet alive, but they spread the word of new, valuable strikes along Fortymile; information that reached McQuesten in time for him to bring back additional supplies.

By the summer of 1887, Fortymile was a crowded waterway—between 200 and 300 men panned the rich river. Americans and Canadians were joined by Scots, Irish, Englishmen, Swedes, Norwegians, Russians, Germans, Swiss, and Australians, and each worked his portion of the diggings along the river. Many of them were washed-out prospectors from other strikes in the lower 48 states. They often had colorful names—Salt Water Jack, Squaw Cameron, Jimmy the Pirate, Buckskin Miller, Pete the Pig—sometimes to disguise their true identities, in case they were wanted for a past crime or were escaping some other aspect of their past lives. Many of the men were known for their quirks and odd natures, which explained some of their monikers. One unique miner was called Cannibal Ike by his associates, because of his practice of "hacking off great slabs of moose meat with his knife and stuffing them into his mouth raw."[49]

(continued on page 62)

THE LEGENDARY TREK OF TOM WILLIAMS

After years of smaller strikes and near misses by gold seekers in the Yukon River region, prospectors finally hit pay dirt in 1886. The entrepreneurs Leroy McQuesten and Arthur Harper knew that the discoveries made by prospectors during the 1886 season would lure additional numbers of miners in search of riches into their part of the Yukon woods. At the end of the digging season, McQuesten set out for San Francisco to get supplies to help stock the shelves of his trading post for the next year.

After McQuesten left for California, Harper hired a pair of prospectors to dig along the banks of the Fortymile River—yet another largely untapped tributary of the Yukon. Harper had already examined some lengths of the Fortymile himself, but his gamble paid off when those he sent out found "good coarse gold that rattled in the pan, the kind every miner seeks."* With these additional late-season strikes on the Fortymile, Harper knew that the news would attract an even greater number of prospectors in 1887. Suddenly, the backwoods entrepreneur became desperate to get word to McQuesten to order even more supplies, including food, for the flock of miners expected the following season.

Winter had already set in along the Yukon, though, and travel was hazardous, even dangerous. Harper offered "good pay and grub to any man who would try to reach Dyea Inlet,"** the location of the port of Skagway, from where a message could be sent to McQuesten before he left San Francisco. The offer was accepted by a prospector from Fort Nelson, a miner who would become legendary—Tom Williams.

Williams left the Yukon region and headed south on December 1, 1886, with an 18-year-old Indian named Bob. His mission would require him to cover 500 miles of a frigid, wintry Alaskan landscape. The journey included traveling up the Yukon River to its headwaters and then crossing a mountain range and glacier field to the open, coastal waters of the Alaskan panhandle. The trip was easy in the beginning; Williams and his companion experienced unseasonably warm temperatures and covered 25 miles on some days. Rains set in after a week, however, slowing their progress. Next, the men faced difficult pack ice. On December 11, Williams noted in his diary: "Traveled all day through heavy pack ice, making only about 10 miles. If the ice continues in our road, we will have a long, weary trip."*** Then, by the end of the second week, Williams' sled broke, requiring them to stop and carry out repairs.

The third week proved extremely difficult. On December 17, the warm winter temperatures melted the surface river ice and Williams' Indian companion fell through the ice into the frigid waters. This happened again over the next several days, leaving Bob nearly frozen to death from repeated exposure to the icy Yukon waters. As they continued, Williams and Bob were forced to leave the river, which had become too dangerous, and continue their journey on land. This required them to carry, or portage, their supplies and sled along the river's banks. By January 1, 1887, the two men, exhausted, reached Lake Laberge, one of the sources of the Yukon River. With the lake frozen solid, Williams and his companion made progress across the lake but, in their rush, failed to rest both themselves and their sled dogs adequately. On January 13, Williams' diary noted: "Left one of our dogs behind as it could not follow us, through fatigue. After traveling about 2 miles we had to camp on account of snow storm."[†]

The entry would be Williams' last. After a month and a half in the wintry wilderness, the two travelers soon faced their greatest challenges. Reaching the opposite shores of the inland lake, Williams and Bob continued on toward the mountain pass at Chilkoot. Local Native Americans refused to accompany them, warning the pair that the trail in front of them was treacherous, but Williams refused to stop. Soon, they were engulfed in a great blizzard. Despite the raging snowstorm, the pair attempted to continue, at one point abandoning their sled because their dogs were exhausted. For several days, they fought through blinding snows and frigid temperatures, making little progress on foot and carrying their packs on their weary backs.

Finally, after reaching the summit of Chilkoot Pass, Williams and Bob became trapped in the snow—their dogs were gone and their food supply was exhausted. For five days, they remained immobile, unable to move on, with no food and no way to build a fire. Williams developed pneumonia. Realizing that they could not remain on the summit and survive, Bob carried his sick comrade for most of a week until they reached the base of the pass, where they encountered local Chilkoot Indians, who helped them build a new sled and gave them directions to the coast.

Although Williams had survived long enough to reach the coast and make contact with local prospectors, he died soon after his arrival at Dyea. Before he succumbed, however, the intrepid gold seeker was able to announce the discovery of gold on Fortymile. The message was driven home by Bob, who picked up a handful of beans from a bag in a trading post, and said: "Gold all same like this." [tt]

In the wake of the successful journey, the word soon spread concerning the latest gold strike in the Yukon Valley region. By the following spring and summer, hundreds more Yukon gold seekers were busy panning for treasure along the banks of the Fortymile. As for Bob, he received eight dollars for his exhaustive effort, as well as a collection taken up by the miners at Dyea to help pay for clothing and medicine for the lone survivor of the deadly mission.

[*] Berton, *The Klondike Fever*, 15.
[**] Place, *The Yukon*, 74.
[***] Keith Wheeler, *The Alaskans* (Alexandria, Va.: Time-Life Books, 1977), 71.
[t] Ibid., 72.
[tt] Tappan Adney, *Klondike Stampede* (New York: Harper Brothers, 1900), 238.

(continued from page 59)

The work done by this strange assortment of men was exhausting and backbreaking, but the strikes were abundant and the pay-offs were huge. Those who arrived before the spring thaw had to take special effort just to prepare the hard, frozen ground for digging. Marian T. Place has described their efforts:

At the end of a work day, they lighted fires and kept them burning all night over a patch of ground. In the morning they scraped away the ashes, shoveled off the thawed muck and moved it to a waste dump. Then they cut more wood, rebuilt their fires, and repeated the thawing and cleanup day after day, week after week. Soon the hole in the ground became a shaft ten, twenty, possibly fifty feet deep. If so, the muck was hauled to the surface by means of a simple windlass and bucket. Most miners worked in twos, one shoveling by candlelight at the bottom of the smoky, cold shaft, the other emptying the buckets on the surface. If they were lucky, their shaft exposed a pay streak of gold.[50]

Wrote one miner from Montana: "If one made 10 inches a day by fires and another six inches by picking he was satisfied."[51] When such a hole did not adequately produce "pay dirt," the prospectors would move to another site and begin the laborious process again.

Once the spring thaw came to the Yukon region, the miners along Fortymile and its smaller tributaries could use a water-washing method of prospecting. They built sluices—long, narrow wooden troughs with a flow of river water routed to run constantly along the man-made course of water. The miners nailed wooden cleats, or slats, across the bottom of the sluice, over which the water flowed. Prospectors then tossed in shovelfuls of dirt and, as the water washed the dirt out of the sluice, the heavier material, such as gold, sank to the sluice bottom and collected against the cleats. Miners then removed the gold from the sluice, pocketing their profits.

Throughout the summer of 1887, the prospectors along Fortymile extracted more than $100,000 in gold dust, flakes, and nuggets. Much of the yield was found along two of Fortymile's tributaries, Chicken Creek and Franklin Creek. In all, there were three groups of miners who worked the river-banks of Fortymile and its vicinity, with varying levels of success. Many of the men were able to extract between $10 and $12 in gold during each day of digging, a low-level return. Mining camp prices on all sorts of commodities from shovels to food were often inflated, reducing the rewards of such minor returns. Some of the miners, though, made greater strikes. One gold seeker uncovered 26 ounces of gold during two lucrative hours of labor. Another pocketed a tidy $250 profit in accumu-lated pickings during a single day's work, while Frank Buteau

During the Yukon gold rush, miners used sluices (shown here), which were long, narrow wooden troughs, to separate gold from dirt. Heavier materials such as gold would sink to the bottom and collect against the wooden cleats, or slats, while the dirt would run off.

was rewarded for his efforts that summer when he dug up $3,000 in gold at his claim along "Bonanza Bar," which earned him the nickname "King of the Fortymile."

By midsummer 1887, the miners had been at work for half of the prospecting season and were running low on supplies. Many moved downstream to the mouth of the Fortymile, waiting for the annual arrival of a steamboat containing cargo that would satisfy the miners' needs. By the end of July, after several delays, the steamer arrived, with McQuesten on board, and the boat was cheered by the anxious prospectors "who were starved for news, goods, and food." [52] The reception was joyous and exciting, because the arrival of such supplies could mean the difference between life or death for hundreds of miners working in a remote region where starvation was a possibility:

> [T]he steamer blew its whistle like the band, and we all got out our guns and started shooting. . . . There was no sleep that night, for poor Al Mayo was talked blind. Everybody helped unload the boat. There were lots of willing hands. However, it was not a big load, only about ten tons of flour, beans, bacon, butter, sugar, but no fancy stuff. . . . Everybody got drunk and slept it off the next day.[53]

Arthur Harper was on the scene, setting up shop on the boat's deck and using a packing case as a business counter. Using scales, he weighed out the miners' gold payments for each supply purchase. Within two days of the supply paddleboat's arrival along Fortymile, McQuesten, Mayo, and Harper's makeshift boat store was completely sold out. Fortunately, another steamer laden with 100 tons of supplies reached Fortymile less than two weeks later.

With the success of the 1887 season along Fortymile, several miners remained in the region, hunkering down for the long, subarctic winter. Others, uncertain of their ability to with-stand the season, or those short on supplies, headed downriver, either abandoning Fortymile completely or with intentions of returning the following spring. The gold-prospecting seasons of 1888 and 1889 proved as rewarding as the previous year and hundreds of miners, some veterans of Fortymile and others new to the Yukon region, toiled along the river, finding new strikes. A unique world developed along Fortymile—a strange society based on treasure hunting, remote wilderness survival, and dealing with the harsh, subarctic weather. Although a mining community—also named Fortymile—was developed on Canadian soil, it was an American settlement, with supplies coming from San Francisco and mail bearing U.S. stamps. With each steamboat arrival along the river, more and more signs of civilization appeared in the bustling, hard-edged mining town. Whereas the miners themselves were typically rough-hewn and fairly unrefined individuals, who lived in fetid log shacks that were dank, dark, and dirty, the town of Fortymile became a place of limited "culture" and upper-class amenities:

> There were saloons that contained Chippendale chairs; and stores that . . . dispensed such delicacies as *pâté de foie gras* and tinned plum pudding. There were Shakespeare clubs formed to give play-readings, and a library whose shelves contained books on science and philosophy. There was a dressmaker with the latest Paris fashions, and an opera house with a troupe of San Francisco dance-hall girls, and even a cigar factory, all housed in log buildings strewn helter-skelter along the mudbank above the Yukon, and surrounded by intervening marshland littered with stumps, wood shavings, and tin cans.[54]

Mining camp social life was often centered on saloons and Fortymile was no different. Ten saloons dotted the prospecting community, where shots of watered-down whiskey sold for 50 cents. The miners tended to consume every shipment of whiskey that arrived by steamboat in a short amount of time, leaving the saloons to peddle a second-rate concoction known as hootchinoo. The brew was a mixture of molasses, sugar, and dried fruit that was fermented with sourdough. It was often distilled in empty coal oil cans and, just like the whiskey shots, sold for 50 cents a drink. This potent alcohol was sometimes called "Forty-Rod Whiskey," "because it was supposed to kill a man at that distance."[55]

NEW DISCOVERIES, A NEW COMMUNITY

As the diggings along Fortymile developed with each passing year and the number of miners increased steadily, the prospectors spread out even farther from town, looking for new places to find gold. Similarly, the long-standing partnership between McQuesten, Mayo, and Harper broke up in 1893. Mayo set up shop farther down the Yukon, at the mouth of Minook Creek. Harper, along with another partner, had taken a boat far up the Yukon River and went into business deep inside Canadian territory, establishing two trading posts, one near Fort Selkirk and another at Sixtymile, located 60 miles above Fort Reliance. As for McQuesten, he remained at Fortymile, but his mind was filled with ideas of grandeur.

That year, while in the employ of McQuesten, a pair of mixed Russian-Indian prospectors made a significant gold strike at Birch Creek, a tributary of the Yukon that flowed into the great river's northernmost stretch. The strike was made on Alaskan soil, and McQuesten soon helped found an American settlement in the area to cater to the influx of miners. Because the newly discovered diggings were located near the Arctic Circle, McQuesten called his town Circle City.

Circle City was located approximately 170 miles downstream on the Yukon from Fortymile, at a point where the river reaches the Yukon Flats. The site was chosen strictly for its proximity to the Birch Creek diggings. The region was dull and lacked beautiful scenery. There were huge stretches of sand, a few stands of thin spruce trees, and low-lying marshes everywhere. During the summer, the "mosquitoes [became] so thick that they blotted out the sun, suffocated packhorses by stopping their nostrils, and drove some men insane."[56] Although the town faced the Yukon River, the mining camps were situated some 80 miles from the river, on a stretch of Birch Creek that paralleled the river. Trails were tramped into existence, connecting the mining camps with the developing

Main Street, Circle City, Alaska. Established in 1893 by Leroy "Jack" McQuesten, Circle City became known as the largest log community in the world and the "Paris of Alaska." At its height, the town contained 28 saloons, 8 dance halls, a library, a school, a hospital, and an opera hall.

mining town. For the new Circle City, life along the Alaskan frontier was atypical. The settlement was remote but yet civilized to a degree. The result was a curious mix of prospectors and progress, self-government and self-reliance:

> In its first year [Circle City] had no jail, no courthouse, no lawyers, and no sheriff, yet there was neither lock nor key in the community. It had no post office and no mail service, and a letter might take from two months to a year to reach its destination, arriving crumpled and odorous, impregnated with tar and bacon. It had no taxes and no banks except the saloons, where men kept their money; and the smallest coin in use was a silver dollar. It had no priest, doctor, church, or school, but it

had [men] with Oxford degrees who could recite Greek poetry
when they were drunk. It had no thermometers to measure
the chilling cold, save for the bottles of quicksilver, whisky,
kerosene, and Perry Davis Painkiller which Jack McQuesten set
outside his store and which froze in ascending order.[57]

Birch Creek proved a literal gold mine for both those miners
who chose the site to stake their claims and for McQuesten as
well. The merchant-trader referred to Circle City as the largest
log community in the world, the "Paris of Alaska." He operated
a two-story trading post, the largest log building in Circle City,
topped by a flagpole "whose cross-arm was handily located in
case a hanging should be required."[58] He hired steamboats,
loaded with supplies, to make trips to Circle City four times a
year. As the town's founder, he had measured out and sold the
lots. Although McQuesten was a shrewd investor and business-
man, he was also known for giving credit to miners who found
themselves down on their luck when they were between strikes.
By 1894, prospectors owed him $100,000, but the wily Alaskan
entrepreneur saw it all repaid, because the first prospecting
season along Birch Creek produced a half-million-dollar payout
in gold to its miners.

In just three years, Circle City had become a booming
gold town, boasting 28 saloons and 8 dance halls that provided
entertainment to otherwise lonely gold seekers. There was a
theater, several stores, and a steady population of 1,200 hearty
miners, some of whom brought their wives north into the
Alaskan wilderness. Those miners who made significant strikes
helped fund the building of a hospital and a library, where
miners could find "the complete works of Huxley, Darwin,
Carlyle, Macaulay, Ruskin, and Irving."[59]

There were dogs everywhere. Many were sled dogs—hearty,
furry huskies and heavy-framed malamutes. Many ran free,
rummaging through garbage and refuse in search of food.

Uncared for, many hungrily devoured miners' boots and leather gloves, horse harnesses, and paste pots. Miners had to build log caches on stilts to keep their supplies away from hungry dogs, "whose teeth could tear open a can of salmon as easily as if it were a paper package."[60] Some miners even swore that some dogs "could tell a tin of marmalade from one of bully beef by a glance at the label."[61]

For a mining town, filled with every facet of society, including gamblers, prostitutes, and hustlers, Circle City was a law-abiding community in a part of Alaska where there were few law officers. A miner's association maintained control over the gold camps and, when U.S. tax collectors reached the remote but wealthy mining town, the prospectors, nearly to the last man, dutifully and patriotically paid their taxes.

By 1897, McQuesten was the wealthiest man in Circle City, perhaps in the entire Yukon region. Circle City was growing and the miners arrived each year in greater numbers, and in 1887 gold strikes reached $1 million. The entire future of the Yukon Valley seemed centered in one place, and McQuesten saw a bright future for his remote Alaskan town; one that was paved in gold. That year, though, new strikes were being made 200 miles upriver, signaling a shift in fortune for those already living in the vicinity of the Yukon River and for tens of thousands more who would soon flock to the area. By 1897, the word "Klondike" would never be spoken of in the same way. (For additional information on the "Paris of Alaska," enter "Circle City, Alaska" into any search engine and browse the many sites listed.)

6

The Klondike Gold Rush

Robert Henderson was the son of a Nova Scotia lighthouse keeper who, as a teenager, had become obsessed with the idea of finding gold. He was a tall, thin man in his late thirties, with a "gaunt hawk's face, fiercely knit brows, and piercing eyes,"[62] and for more than 20 years, he had searched the world over, from Australia to Canada, in search of the precious metal. In 1894, while Circle City was being settled, he was already in Alaska, along with several fellow prospectors, poling a boat along the Yukon River hundreds of miles to the north. The Fortymile was largely already staked out, claimed by hundreds of would-be miners. Henderson and his friends decided to try their luck where few had bothered to search. After panning along the Pelly River and finding little metal, Henderson and his friends reached a trading post at the mouth of the Sixtymile River, a store owned by two other prospectors, the aforementioned Arthur Harper and Joseph Ladue. With Harper away from the post, Ladue, a dark-skinned Frenchman who had been on the Sixtymile since 1882, greeted Henderson and his companions, who were already contemplating abandoning the Yukon Valley; their prospecting efforts having proved fruitless.

During a conversation with the new arrivals, Ladue offered to stake the men if they would prospect near his post, situated 100 miles up the Yukon from Fortymile. Any significant gold strike would lure a wave of gold seekers, which would provide a boost for Ladue's trading efforts. Henderson's companions were through with the Yukon, however; they were ready to return to Colorado, where they had already searched for gold. As for Henderson, he was ready to give the local rivers a try. Ladue pointed him toward the untested banks of a local tributary, Indian River, 30 miles from Ladue's post. For the next two years Henderson searched the Indian River and its tributaries for gold.

During those years, the Nova Scotia native did find trace amounts of gold, but the riches he had spent most of his life searching for continued to elude him. His panning produced enough gold to keep Henderson in supplies and little more. Then, on a warm August day in 1896, Henderson climbed a small mountain called the Dome. Several creeks that reached Indian River flowed down the Dome's flanks. Henderson speculated that additional creeks on the back side of the Dome flowed into another river, the Thron-diuck, which local miners often mispronounced as the "Klondike." Determined to know for certain, Henderson scaled the bald mountain. At the summit, he saw the rivers he had envisioned and "a great plateau creased and gouged and furrowed by centuries of running water."[63] These feeder streams for the Klondike soon became the focus of Henderson's ongoing quest for gold.

He walked to the nearest creek, waded out into its waters, and scooped up a pan of gravel, just as he had done countless times before. This time, however, bits of gold appeared. A mile downstream, several pans yielded an average of a half-dollar's worth of gold. Continuing to work the feeder streams for a few weeks, Henderson panned $750 in gold flakes, more than an average Yukon miner dug up in a year. He was forced to break off his efforts to return to Ladue's trading post for more supplies, where he gave the Frenchman the good news.

On returning to his newly found stake, Henderson happened to meet up with a local hunter, George Carmack, and two of Carmack's fellow hunters, a pair of Indians known as Skookum Jim and Tagish Charlie. Carmack's father had been a prospector in the gold camps of the 1849 California gold rush, and George was born near San Francisco. At age 16, he had set out for Alaska on a ferryboat, but he had never developed an interest in gold seeking, instead wanting to live with local Indians, from whom he learned the art of hunting. Even though Carmack and the Indians were not prospectors, Henderson told them about his newfound discovery. Despite the hopeful news, the three hunters did not immediately join Henderson. After a few days, with dreams of gold and easy pickings, Carmack and his Indian friends decided to hike over to Henderson's camp. The three men did not follow the river but headed up the valley of Rabbit Creek, poling a canoe up the Klondike River for two miles, and then hiking overland to the mouth of Rabbit Creek to try their hunters' hands at prospecting. They found some gold, but continued to move on to other creeks and rivers until they reached Henderson's camp.

After reaching Henderson's claim, the anxious prospector and the Indians had an argument over Henderson's refusal to sell them some tobacco. The clash caused Carmack and his friends to leave Henderson and to set out in search of their own diggings—and they found gold immediately. As they moved from stream to stream, the gold was almost constant. After several days, the three prospectors found themselves back on Rabbit Creek, and they camped along the waterway on August 16, 1896. The next 24 hours would dramatically change their lives and the history of the Yukon.

The stories of their great gold discoveries along Rabbit Creek do not correspond. According to Carmack's version, he claims to have found the first big nugget along the creek. Skookum Jim and Tagish Charlie claimed that Jim had produced the first significant find while Carmack was asleep under a tree. Jim had just shot a moose and was "cleaning a dishpan in the creek and made the find"—a gold nugget as large as a man's thumb.[64] Jim shouted for his comrades and soon the three men were squatting in Rabbit Creek, scooping up pans of gold-littered gravel, with the average pan yielding $4 in gold. (If a miner's pan produced 10 cents in gold, that was considered a good find.) Carmack claims he saw "the raw gold laying thick between flaky slabs like cheese sandwiches. . . . I felt as if I just dealt myself a royal flush in the game of life."[65] The three prospectors were certain that they had stumbled on a find of incredible proportions and, indeed, they had. Within a hundred

The White Pass Chronicle announces the discovery of gold during the Klondike gold rush of the summer of 1897. By mid-July 1897, the first boat from the Yukon region, the *Excelsior*, arrived in San Francisco carrying a cargo of $400,000 in Klondike gold.

yards from where they were standing in the waters of Rabbit Creek lay millions of dollars worth of gold. They each began to whoop and holler and engage in a dance of joy that Carmack later described as a "combination Scottish hornpipe, Indian fox trot, syncopated Irish jig, and Siwash hula." [66]

By the following day, August 17, the three men officially staked their claims. By Canadian law, a prospector could only make one claim in any given mining district. Carmack took his axe and blazed a flat cut on a small spruce tree, where he wrote:

TO WHOM IT MAY CONCERN

I do, this day, locate and claim, by right of discovery, five hundred feet, running up stream from this notice. Located this 17th day of August, 1896. *(G.W. Carmack)* [67]

From the discovery site, Carmack stepped off his stake, which he called *One Below*, because it was located downstream from the point of discovery. Tagish Charlie staked out *Two Below*, and Skookum Jim laid claim to *One Above*.

Once their claims were secure, the three prospectors began telling their story of newly discovered and rich diggings along Rabbit Creek. It was common practice among miners and prospectors to share information and good fortune with their fellow gold seekers. Carmack did not take the time to inform Henderson of his findings, however, probably because of Henderson's abrupt behavior with his Indian friends. Soon, miners flocked to Rabbit Creek and were sharing in the riches. Rabbit Creek was renamed "Bonanza Creek," after a Spanish word meaning "source of wealth." A genuine gold rush was in the making:

> Up and down the Yukon Valley the news spread like a great stage-whisper. It moved as swiftly as the breeze in the birches, and more mysteriously. Men squatting by nameless creeks heard the tale, dropped their pans, and headed for the Klondike. Men seated by dying campfires heard it and started up in the night, shrugging off sleep to make tracks for the new strike. Men poling up the Yukon toward the mountains or drifting down the Yukon toward the wilderness heard it and did an abrupt about-face in the direction of the salmon stream whose name no one could pronounce properly. Some did not hear the news at all, but, drifting past the Klondike's mouth, saw the boats and the tents and the gesticulating figures, felt the hair rise on their napes . . . and joined the clamoring throng pushing up . . . Rabbit Creek.[68]

FOUNDING THE TOWN OF DAWSON CITY

Within just five days of Carmack's claim and his news that there was an abundance of gold along Rabbit Creek, the region was

After gold was discovered at nearby Rabbit Creek in August 1896, Dawson City seemingly sprang up over night. By 1898, the town of nearly 40,000 inhabitants had such amenities as running water, steam heat, electricity, and even telephone lines.

filling up with miners. Joe Ladue, the store proprietor who had convinced Henderson to try his hand along the Klondike, scrambled into the region—not to prospect but to establish a supply store and to stake out a town site at the foot of the Dome, near the Klondike's mouth. Here, he would make his true fortune because by 1898, "lots sold for as much as five thousand dollars a front foot on the main street" [69] in the mining community that Ladue would name Dawson City, after the director of Canada's Geographical Survey, a geologist named George M. Dawson. Officers of the Canadian Mounted Police arrived on the scene early, ensuring law and order in the bustling gold camp. Sanitation at the new site was an immediate problem, one Ladue addressed by building two large public outhouses. Soon,

GEORGE CARMACK, TAGISH CHARLIE, AND SKOOKUM JIM: THE REST OF THEIR STORY

The great Klondike gold rush was generally credited to the discoveries made that summer day in August 1896 by George Washington Carmack, Tagish Charlie, and Skookum Jim, his two Native comrades. That the three men prospered is without dispute, and their discoveries changed their lives—but how much? What happened to these three men who discovered the first nuggets in a strike that would yield millions in profits for countless miners who followed in their footsteps? Their story is one of success and tragedy.

Immediately following their success in the newly discovered gold fields, the three men enjoyed high times and took their wives on a shopping spree to Seattle, "where they delighted in throwing money out of their hotel windows." They returned to their diggings, though, and unearthed thousands more in gold. Their source of wealth seemed unlimited.

Although it was never known how much Carmack profited from his first claim on Rabbit Creek, he became wealthy enough to leave the gold camps in 1898, along with his Native American wife, Kate, and a daughter, with plans to tour the world. Instead, though, Carmack and his family went to California, where they stayed with his sister. By 1899, he went back to the gold fields, leaving his family behind with his sister—but he never returned to them, instead taking up with another woman, Marguerite Laimee.

Laimee was a dance hall girl who had worked in saloons in the gold fields of South Africa and Australia. By 1900, the couple left Dawson City and married. They moved to Seattle, taking the wealth Carmack had accumulated

Dawson City was a thriving, stinking settlement—like many of the small towns scattered across the American West.

Before the end of August, the entire length of Bonanza (Rabbit) Creek, a distance of 15 miles, had been claimed and staked out. As for Carmack, he continued to work his claim but was immediately sidetracked by lack of money for supplies and lost time having to cut logs for Ladue's sawmill to earn enough money to feed himself. Within the first month following his official claim in mid-August, though, he had managed to build sluices that in the gold fields and the money Marguerite had earned as a camp follower. (She left Dawson with $55,000 of her own profits.) Carmack made additional monies investing in Seattle real estate, including a hotel and an apartment house. He also operated a mine in California. The two lived happily together until Carmack's death in 1922.

As for Charlie and Jim, their stories were mixed with wealth and tragedy. Tagish Charlie sold out his mining claims in 1901 and lived the remainder of his life at Carcross, a settlement upstream on the Yukon. He lived well, operated a hotel, and spent money lavishly, including buying diamond earrings for his daughter. Many of those around him forgot he was an Indian and treated him as they would a wealthy white man. He indulged in heavy drinking, though, and, on a warm summer's day, while drunk, fell from a footbridge and drowned.

Skookum Jim did not sell his claims but leased them out for years, collecting annual royalties of $90,000, but he was not a happy man. Just as George Carmack had longed for years prior to his great gold discovery to be thought of as an Indian, so Jim wanted to be thought of as a white man. He never settled down to enjoy his wealth but continued to live the difficult life of a Yukon prospector, traveling endlessly across the Yukon region in search of greater riches, and sometimes going days without eating. He wore his body out prematurely, weakening himself through his relentless drive and incautious diet. He died, in 1916, still obsessed with the thought of finding more gold.

produced $1,400 in gold. Carmack was on his way to becoming a wealthy man.

Although the onset of a subarctic winter usually signaled the end of prospecting season along the Yukon River, the rumors of great strikes along Bonanza Creek caused miners to flock to Dawson City from as far away as Circle City, 225 miles downstream. By January 1897, the local rush to Dawson was under way. Those receiving word of the strikes from outside the region could not even consider making the expedition north because of the season. Miners packed up their household goods, their shovels and picks, and headed north to Bonanza Creek, dragging it all on snowsleds. There was such a great demand for dogsleds that winter that the price for a sled increased from $50 to more than $200. Those who were able to get a sled but could find no dogs pulled their sleds themselves. By the spring of 1897, with gold fever spreading like wind-driven snow, Circle City was practically abandoned, while Dawson witnessed an influx of 1,500 residents. These were only the advance guard, however; the torrent of miners would not arrive until spring.

THE NEWS SPREADS

The gold rush that occurred in the summer of 1897 would prove to be the richest in the history of the Yukon Valley. Whereas the early prospectors who flocked to the Klondike region were those who were already working the diggings along the Yukon, a great influx of miners from around the world also reached Rabbit Creek and the surrounding streambeds. Word of the rich strikes appears to have reached the outside world by mid-July 1897, when the first boat from the Yukon region, the *Excelsior*, made port at San Francisco carrying a cargo of $400,000 in Klondike gold. When that small steamship reached the California docks, on July 16, there were several new millionaires on board who had been long-time gold seekers in the region but had never struck it rich before. These newly wealthy, "scruffy miners swaggered down the gangplank carrying jars, satchels and cases filled with gold," as 5,000 excited people crowded over the docks, cheering those who had made their fortune.[70] The following day, a second steamer, the *Portland*, reached Seattle from Alaska, with 68 rich miners and a cargo that included a ton of gold.

Newspapers trumpeted the rich strikes along the Klondike, which were no longer the stuff of stories and legend; these gold strikes were real, and there were wealthy miners in the streets of San Francisco to prove it. Reporters interviewed any rich miner who was willing to tell his story. One claimed that the gold in the Klondike was 10 times greater than the amount of gold unearthed during the California gold rush of 1849. Soon, thousands of gold-hungry, first-time prospectors were preparing to make their way to the unknown region of the Yukon River and its tributaries in one of the most frantic gold rushes in U.S. history. The gold rush couldn't have come at a better time. Since 1893, the United States had been in the throes of a severe economic depression, one that left many thousands of Americans unemployed. Factories and mines remained closed; banks had shut their doors. To those struggling through the depression, the lure of treasure for the taking in the frozen North had a strong, irresistible appeal. In such Pacific coastal cities as Seattle, San Francisco, and Portland, even those who were employed—dock hands, shopkeepers, laborers, small businessmen—abandoned their low-paying jobs and set out for Alaska and Yukon Territory.

A strong desire to make one's way to the gold fields of the North was not enough, though. Preparing to move to the Yukon region and to work the gold camps was a complicated and expensive process. Just the cost of getting to the Klondike was high: The average steamship ticket cost a would-be prospector $150. In addition, a ship's captain would charge the miner for hauling supplies and equipment. One such steamer company charged shipping costs of 10 cents per pound and limited the weight to 1,200 pounds. A prospector could wait to buy such supplies until he arrived in the Yukon region, but the costs of such items in the gold camps were exorbitant—much higher than it cost to buy them elsewhere and pay for their shipment.

Supplies for such a venture were also expensive. Those miners who arrived during the summer of 1897 at San Francisco and Seattle provided lists to newspaper reporters of the supplies needed to survive in the subarctic for 18 months. The cost for the enumerated items was nearly $200 and included the following provisions:

- 200 pounds of bacon
- 800 pounds of flour
- 150 pounds of dried fruit (because the average miner's diet was starchy and high in carbohydrates, fruit was an essential health food that encouraged regularity)
- 200 pounds of corn meal
- 50 pounds of rice
- 75 pounds of coffee
- 40 pounds of tea
- 75 pounds of sugar
- 150 pounds of beans
- A case of condensed milk and
- An assortment of dried vegetables and meats.

In addition, the suggested clothing list included two corduroy suits, three pairs of rubber boots (a constant maintenance problem), three pairs of heavy work shoes, three dozen heavy woolen socks, six pairs of woolen mittens, three pairs of woolen gloves, three sets of winter long johns (underwear), two mackinaw suits, two hats, four heavy woolen shirts, one heavy coat, and three pairs of heavy woolen blankets.

Despite the fact that the expenses, which, including food, clothing, supplies, shipping, and passage, might amount to $1,500, approximately 100,000 would-be miners made the trip to the Klondike region from mid-1897 through 1898. Most of them came from the United States and a smaller number from Canada. Some came from as far away as Europe, Asia, and Latin America. Even a group of aboriginal tribesmen, the Maoris, trekked from their homes in New Zealand.

There were teachers, fishermen, city clerks, small-town politicians, Civil War veterans, former Indian scouts, and even an English aristocrat, Lord Avenmore, who reached the Klondike with several servants in tow. Although most of those who headed in a rush to the Yukon Territory were men, there were women as well. When the steamer *Portland* left Seattle a week after delivering rich miners from the Yukon region, the 85 passengers onboard included 15 women, nearly all of whom were single and unescorted. As a Seattle newspaper reported, "women are among the adventuring travelers."[71]

MAKING THE TRIP NORTH
By early September 1897, six weeks after the arrival of the *Portland* in Seattle, 9,000 excited gold seekers had booked passage and were on their way on various ships, along with 36,000 tons of supplies and food, horses, and sled dogs. Some of those who traveled north had experience working gold fields in Colorado, California, and elsewhere, but nearly all of them had never been to Yukon Territory or Alaska. In fact, approximately half of them never reached the gold camps.

Those ships that steamed toward Alaskan waters were typically bound for one of two northern ports—St. Michael, the old Inuit settlement and former Russian fur-trading community at the mouth of the Yukon River on the western shores of Alaska, or Skagway, situated along the southern Alaska coast. Once they reached the mouth of the Yukon, the prospectors would take passage on a paddle-wheel steamboat, and then make a 2,000-mile excursion up the Yukon River to the vicinity of the gold camps in Yukon Territory. The trip from Seattle to St. Michael and up the river took one-and-a-half months. Although this was an all-water route, requiring virtually no overland hiking, the Yukon could only be traversed between May and September, when the river had thawed enough and winter freezes were no longer a threat.

The passage to Skagway was the more popular route. It was cheaper and could be made at any time of the year. That August, steamships left such Pacific ports as Seattle; San Francisco; and Victoria, British Columbia; bound for Skagway. From Seattle, a steamship took five days to cover the 1,000 miles to the Alaskan port. Beyond the coastal port, the route to the Klondike was a rugged, overland trek that included crossing the Coast Mountains, plus another 550 miles over difficult terrain to Dawson City. This portion of the trip to reach the riches of Bonanza Creek was arduous, daunting, and even deadly.

At best, the trail to Dawson City and the gold fields was backbreaking. With more than a half-ton of supplies to carry, miners were forced to cover the same ground on multiple trips, because carrying their entire load of supplies at one time was impossible. One of the early, "outsider" arrivals to the Klondike was Jack London, who later became a famous American author and novelist. In his journal, London explained the difficulties of the 33-mile overland trek from Dyea Trail, or Chilkoot Trail, to Lake Lindeman:

> I expect to carry 100 lbs. To the load on good trail & on the worst, 75 lbs. That is, for every mile to the lakes, I will have to travel from 20 to 30 miles. I have 1000 lbs. In my outfit. I have to divide it into from 10 to fifteen loads according to the trail. I take a load a mile & come back empty that makes two miles . . . Am certain we will reach the lake in 30 days.[72]

In the early days of the Klondike gold rush, the prospectors who left from Skagway used the Skagway Trail through White Pass, a 45-mile-long rugged route that was barely passable, sometimes narrowing to a few feet as it hugged the banks of the Skagway River. It was a difficult course—"a zigzagging, roller-coasting, switchbacking route through hill and canyon, mountain and valley"—that passed through thick woods, marshes, and hard rock hills.[73] Many of the miners brought horses to the trail, intending to use them as pack animals, but the horses were often unaccustomed to such difficult work and many simply fell along the trail and were abandoned. By the fall of 1897, Skagway Trail was littered with the rotting carcasses of 2,000 horses, giving the route a new name: "Dead Horse Trail." To make travel on the trail even more difficult that autumn, rains fell almost constantly and in great sheets.

There was an alternate route to the Skagway Trail known as the Dyea Trail. The Skagway Trail was 10 miles longer than the Dyea, but it passed through an elevation 600 feet lower. From the fall through the winter of 1897–1898, 22,000 prospectors hiked the Dyea Trail, about half of those who headed out of Skagway to the North. The most daunting portion of the trail was known as Chilkoot Pass because of its longtime use by the Chilkoot Indians. Also known as the "Scales," because the gold seekers weighed their supplies at its base, Chilkoot was a steep rise, a "sheer, thousand-foot hill where, in the winter, fifteen hundred steps were cut in the frozen snow."[74] The steps were often referred to by Klondikers as "the Golden Stairs." Miners who scaled the pass carrying just 50 pounds of supplies took six hours, on average, to reach the summit. With hundreds of pounds of supplies to transport over the pass, prospectors had to make at least several dozen trips, sometimes requiring weeks. Members of the Canadian North West Mounted Police oversaw the site, ushering those Klondikers who completed the gauntlet of the pass through a Canadian checkpoint. These stern-minded Mounties typically refused anyone the privilege of crossing over Chilkoot Pass until they had hauled at least six months of supplies up the mountain. Beyond the pass, the gold seekers continued on the Dyea Trail for another 17 miles to Lake Bennett. (For additional information on this route to the Yukon, enter "Chilkoot Trail" into any search engine and browse the many sites listed.)

This lake was connected to Lake Lindeman by a waterway known as One Mile River, where the Skagway Trail ended.

Dyea Trail, also known as Chilkoot Trail, was the 33-mile overland route to the gold fields of the Yukon. Twenty-two thousand prospectors hiked this treacherous trail between the fall of 1897 and the winter of 1898.

These lakes serve as the headwaters of the Yukon River. During that anxious fall of 1897, the Klondikers had to remain on the lakes due to the onset of winter, when the lakes and the river were frozen over. By the following spring, after spending the winter building boats for themselves and their supplies, the miners headed down the Yukon River by the thousands. They would have to traverse 550 miles on the river to Dawson City, a voyage that took two weeks.

By late May 1898, a great flotilla of prospectors began to float down the Yukon, including thousands of boats, canoes, and rafts—15,000 people and 30 million pounds of supplies and equipment. The river narrowed between sheer cliff walls at Miles Canyon, where the caravan encountered dangerous whitewater. Along the canyon, 150 boats capsized or crashed onto the rocks, killing 10 prospective miners. The disaster led the Northwest Mounted Police to establish a checkpoint on the river above Miles Canyon to stop boats from being overloaded, which greatly reduced the number of wrecks and mishaps.

LIFE IN THE MINING TOWN OF DAWSON

When the great influx of tens of thousands of prospectors reached Dawson, the mining town was only two years old. Suddenly, this newest Yukon Territory mining community was overrun with treasure seekers, most of whom had no experience prospecting. By the spring of 1898, the city was home to more than 20,000 people. The remote Yukon town lacked many of the amenities common to late-nineteenth-century American life, but there was one element of modernity that Dawson had plenty of—money, mostly in the form of gold dust, flakes, and nuggets. Back in the United States, the average worker earned less than two dollars a day. In Dawson, even the lowliest jobs paid quite well. Gold dust weighers earned $20, wagon masters were paid $100 for their efforts, and lawyers could ask $150 for their services—all in a day's work. Even washerwomen were adequately paid, and after laundering miners' clothes for a full day, they might scoop up $20 in gold dust from the bottoms of their washtubs.

Everybody paid for nearly everything in gold dust, even though Canadian dollars were available at two local banks. At many places of business, the owner weighed out gold dust on his own counter scales, with an ounce being worth approximately $16. With so much money on the streets of Dawson

City, the mining community experienced almost immediate inflation. When a new resident arrived with a cow, because of the scarcity of dairy products, thirsty miners willingly paid $30 a gallon for milk. A shrewd entrepreneur arrived with 2,400 eggs and promptly sold them for $1.50 apiece. When someone reached the boisterous mining town with several cages of cats, he could ask $15 apiece for them, and lonely miners eagerly paid up.

Dawson not only grew quickly in population; by 1899, the town had running water, steam heat, and electricity. Even telephone lines had been strung to the far-flung capital of the Klondike gold rush. Restaurants served exotic foods and wines, delivered up the Yukon River on paddle wheelers that arrived with greater regularity with each passing month. Despite the number of saloons and gambling houses in the town, life in Dawson was usually tame, with the majority of its citizens law-abiding. The Northwest Mounted Police, the Mounties, were a constant presence, and they helped keep peace and order in the mining town. All handguns had to be licensed. There were very few murders (only two in Dawson in 1898) and the most common crime was petty theft, which included dog stealing. When a thief was caught, conviction might lead to a punishment of chopping wood to provide heat for the town's government buildings. Centered in the midst of a hostile and primitive world, Dawson City became a model of civility and safety.

A SHORT-LIVED RUSH

The year 1898 was a bonanza for the Klondikers. They fanned out along dozens of feeder creeks and streams of the Klondike River, as well as the Yukon River, and found more gold than many had ever imagined. Between July and November of that year, the U.S. mints in San Francisco and Seattle received approximately $10 million in gold from the Klondike region.

The following year, 1899, an additional $16 million was delivered, and 1900 witnessed another $22 million being received by the two mints. Although the vast majority of gold seekers arrived in the Klondike region through 1898, the gold rush, despite the riches it produced, did not last long. Millions of dollars of flakes and nuggets, as well as whole veins of gold, were unearthed by thousands of miners but, by the summer of 1900, the gold rush had run its course.

During the short-lived rush, Dawson City had grown to a population of 40,000. Before the rush was over, the Canadian government officially created Yukon Territory from the immense western province, Northwest Territories. Dawson became the territorial capital and remained the center of territorial government until the 1950s.

Gold prospecting did not grind to an immediate halt, however, with the arrival of the new century. For the next 50 years, following the discoveries by George Carmack, Tagish Charlie, and Skookum Jim, the Klondike region produced a half-billion dollars worth of gold, much of that unearthed through large-scale corporate mining. By that time, the day of the lone prospector had nearly become part of an already legendary era in the history of the Yukon River valley.

7

Paddle Wheelers on the Yukon

W ith the tremendous influx of prospectors into the regions of the Klondike and Yukon Rivers, the history of Alaska and the Yukon Territory was changed forever. Throughout the nineteenth century leading up to the 1896–1898 gold rush, the non-Indian population of the region had remained few and scattered, centered largely in those intrepid extensions of various fur companies. With few people reaching the region prior to the Klondike gold rush of the 1890s, the need for extensive transportation systems across the subarctic region remained too expensive and even unnecessary. As the gold rush drew 100,000 people to the waters of the Yukon River and its tributaries, however, the rivers themselves became extensive highways, bustling with a new type of transportation—the great paddle-wheel steamboats—that dominated the comings and goings of many in Alaska and Yukon Territory.

EARLY STEAMERS ON THE YUKON

The earliest steamboats on the Yukon predated the Klondike gold rush by several decades. In 1866, the men laying the line for the Russian-American Telegraph Company delivered a small, steam-powered boat to the Yukon, the *Wilder*, which plied the waters of the lower river. Other early steamboats soon followed, largely for use by various fur-trading companies in the region. These included the *Yukon*, a boat of the Alaska Commercial Company, in 1869; the Western Fur and Trading Company's *St. Michael*, introduced a decade later; and the *New Racket*, another Alaska Commercial Company steamer that arrived on the Yukon in 1882.

Although these earliest steamboats were used by fur companies doing business in Alaska, other steamers were introduced to the Yukon during the first significant gold strikes that led up to the great Klondike discoveries of the late 1890s. When gold was discovered at Fortymile River in 1886, a mining town developed at its confluence with the Yukon. A few years later,

Circle City, situated 170 miles downriver from Fortymile, came into being because of the gold rush. As other towns sprang up, the need for delivering supplies up the Yukon became a driving force for the North American Trading and Transportation Company to deliver a steamboat, the *PB Weare*, into service on the Yukon by 1892. These early steamers proved more ideal than any other type of craft on the Yukon. The current of the great subarctic river was always strong and passage upriver was too difficult for almost all other types of boats. In addition, these draft boats could ply the waters of a wide number of tributaries of the Yukon; while other boats found it harder to navigate those waters because they were too shallow.

The number of steam-powered paddle wheelers on the Yukon remained inconsequential, however, until the great gold strikes of the late 1890s. With a sudden need to transport tens of thousands of gold seekers to remote camps in the Alaska-Yukon interior, the number of steamboats suddenly swelled. Many of those early arrivals reached the Klondike by way of southern Alaskan coastal towns such as Skagway and Dyea at the head of the Inside Passage. They hiked over the passes leading into British Columbia to Lake Bennett and then took small boats down the Yukon for 500 miles, until they reached the town of Dawson in the midst of the newly discovered gold fields.

The steamboats offered another alternative—one that was longer but infinitely less grueling. Prospectors took passage on an ocean-going steamer and arrived at the western port of St. Michael, near the mouth of the Yukon River. Then they booked a berth on one of a number of steam paddle wheelers. The trip from St. Michael to Dawson covered hundreds of miles of the Yukon River and took several weeks, but the trip involved fewer hazards and physical challenges.

As the gold rush unfolded, the demand for steamboats on the Yukon surpassed the number of available boats. By 1897, however, 30 new steamboat companies were doing business along the river, alongside the veteran steamers that belonged to the Alaska Commercial Company and the North American Trading and Transportation Company. All up and down the Pacific Coast, from California to Washington, shipyards were busy building new steamers for service to Alaskan waters. Before the arrival of the railroad in the Alaskan interior, the only available means of getting a steamboat constructed on the West Coast was to steam it or tow it across 2,500 miles of open Pacific waters to St. Michael and then take the boat upriver 2,000 miles to the gold camps, such as Whitehorse. By the summer of 1898, more than 110 paddle-wheel steamboats were in use along the Lower Yukon River alone. By the turn of the century, the number had more than doubled. The great era of steamboating on the Yukon was hitting its stride.

A BOAT DESIGNED FOR THE YUKON

There was no better watercraft than the paddleboat of the late nineteenth century to provide the necessary elements of transport needed for use on the Yukon River. In his book, *Paddlewheelers of Alaska and the Yukon*, Graham Wilson described the essential qualities of these masters of the great northern river:

> In many ways the paddlewheeler was the perfect craft to navigate the Yukon River. These ships were carefully designed and adapted to the often harsh northern conditions. Paddlewheeler designs varied widely depending on the cargo they were intended to carry, the nature of the river and the fashions of the day when they were built. The goal was to build a hull which could support the greatest weight on the shallowest draft while allowing for speed and maneuverability. The paddlewheelers of the Yukon were built with the sand and gravel bars of the Yukon River in mind and tended to have a shallow draft, with a long, wide, flat hull and no keel.[75]

Many of the earliest steamboats built for the Yukon had been designed after the typical Mississippi River model, boats that were built for a slow-moving river, not for the fast, shifting currents and narrow chutes and channels of the great northern river. Boat builders soon determined, through trial and experience, that they would have to design slightly different boats for use on the Yukon, because of its peculiar tendencies and unique subarctic qualities. To allow for greater stability in swifter currents, and to keep the Alaskan models from sagging, the new Yukon boats featured a "hog chain," which was attached from the boat's bow to its stern. The chain could be tightened, which would cause an equal tightening of the hull, and the chain could be loosened according to the weight of the load on board or even the physical conditions of the river during each season or regional leg.

In many aspects of design and construction, the Yukon paddle wheelers looked similar to the steamers common to rivers across the United States in the late nineteenth century. Most were designed for hauling a large amount of freight. Some of the largest steamers plying Alaskan waters were designed to haul 300 tons of freight and 150 passengers. The cargo deck was established on the boat's first level, near the water line, to help ease the loading and unloading of the freight. In addition, the boat's boiler and machinery were also located on the first deck. The next deck up was the saloon or passenger deck. Most of the boat's passenger cabins were located there, along with the dining rooms; toilet facilities; galley, where the cooking took place; and some of the crew's quarters. This deck served as the center for most of the social activity on the steamer. In most Yukon boats, the passenger rooms did not feature running water but a washstand with a water basin and pitcher instead. The hot water used in cooking was provided by the boat's boiler on the first deck. The typical galley included an icebox, where perishable foods were stored.

(In the subarctic, there was ice available from many icehouses along the river.) Above the passenger deck was the "Texas Deck," a name that identified the deck with the largest and better quality cabins; these were generally used by the boat's captain and his officers. (The name "Texas Deck" originated during Mississippi riverboat days, when passenger cabins were named for states in the Union—for example, Ohio, Alabama, Missouri—and this gave rise to the term "staterooms.")

To provide power for these great wooden freighters of the North, the Yukon boats featured a locomotive boiler system, large steam-driven pistons that moved both the immense paddle system as well as the loading winches on deck. With so much wood available along the river, the Yukon steamers did not need to carry much wood, which would have needlessly increased the weight on the boats and the number of times a boat was required to "wood up," or stop for local woodchoppers to bring on more wood for fuel. These great western steamers consumed enormous amounts of wood, perhaps as much as a cord of wood an hour. Wood camps along the river soon became a common sight. Some of the later steamboat models were converted to oil burners and a few burned coal as fuel, but coal was not readily available in Alaska along the Yukon.

The great system of propulsion featured on the nineteenth-century steamboats were the paddle wheels: giant, circular, wooden frames that stood as high as 20 feet and often measured 20 feet from starboard to port at the stern of a boat. They were a simple series of wooden paddles, flat-board planks that turned into the water and propelled the craft forward, whether traveling with or against a river's current. The long paddle wheels were turned over by large metal extensions, called pitman arms, which were attached to the paddle wheel on one end and the steam engines on the other. As the boat's boilers produced steam, they provided the energy to operate the engine that moved the pitman arms. Hundreds of horsepower were required to turn the giant paddle wheels. At the center base of the stern, a rudder enabled the pilot to turn the boat to the left or right in a long sweep across a body of water. Such turns could not be completed quickly and required a wide berth on a river.

A SEASONAL MEANS OF TRAVEL

On rivers in the American South and Southwest, nineteenth-century paddle-wheel steamers could ply up and down rivers throughout the year. On the Yukon River, however, the steamboat transport season was limited to only part of the year. For months during the winter, the Yukon and its tributaries might freeze solid on the surface, making steamboat or any other type of boat navigation on such rivers impossible. How soon the river might thaw out adequately each spring for steamboat passage, or how early the winter freeze locked the river's waters in ice, sometimes dramatically affected the profit margins of steamboat companies. A typical season often opened in mid-to-late May and continued until early October. Sometimes boat owners used various techniques to break up the ice on the river:

> Lake Laberge was one of the last stretches on the river to thaw and Herbert Wheeler, then president of the White Pass Company, devised a unique method to speed the breakup. Using a Model T truck, he spread a mixture of carbon black, old crankcase oil, and diesel oil in a 60-foot side path across the length of the lake. The mixture absorbed the sun's rays and rotted the ice. Steamers pushing barges could break up the ice and add perhaps several weeks to the season.[76]

Alaska ice posed one of the most serious problems a Yukon River steamboat might face. Even following the spring breakup of the ice that sheathed the river through the winter months, paddle wheelers might encounter massive ice chunks floating in the river. During late fall navigation, boats could become locked in ice as the river's surface froze as a result of a long night of below freezing temperatures. Such ice was dangerous to a boat, because the hulls were wooden. Some boats were protected by iron-plated hulls but that only added weight to the steamer. Sometimes, rolling masses of ice were known to push against a boat so severely that it rammed the hapless craft against a rocky shore or against other boats tied up at the same river wharf or even managed to drive a boat ashore. Navigating a paddle wheeler on the Yukon was an experience that featured unique dangers.

As an unpredictable winter approached each year, steamboat pilots often raced against time and nature to bring the navigation season to a close and dock their boats for the winter before a permanent freeze. If a boat's captain did not order his boat to dock in time, and ice forced the steamer to a standstill in the river, the craft had to be abandoned for the winter. Occasionally, such trapped boats were crushed by the winter ice and destroyed. For those boats winched out of the river to safety in dry dock, the winter season provided an opportunity for maintenance crews to carry out boat inspections and repairs in preparation for another season of hauling freight and passengers along the Yukon. On the Lower Yukon, steamers were often dry-docked at St. Michael; along the coast, at Nenana; or at a few other river sites. On the Upper Yukon, the Whitehorse and Dawson boatyards were commonly used.

THE PERILS OF YUKON STEAMBOATING

The threat of the onset of winter ice represented just one of the many difficulties, challenges, and disasters a steamboat on the Yukon River might face during each year of service. Even the most experienced boat pilots never took the Yukon for granted, because the river harbored many natural obstacles. One constant challenge was the river's current. The Yukon is a swift-flowing river, moving at a speed of five or six miles an hour. The speed of the river always made upriver navigation difficult as a boat fought against the current, but when passing downriver, the river could sweep a boat onto an obstacle or barrier before the pilot had time to react. The Yukon was unchanneled—a natural river whose course was marked by narrow channels and rapids. Along the lower portion of the river, where the Yukon passed through lowlands, the great Alaskan waterway had a tendency to meander. Meandering is a natural tendency of all rivers that pass through flat country. Overflows and bank erosion often cause a river to create new and multiple channels, as the river fingers its way along, seeking new directions.

As a boat passed through a region of meandering multi-channels, boat pilots had to be especially cautious as they selected the best channel for navigation. A wrong decision might land a boat on a sandbar, or cause it to strike a submerged obstacle such as an unseen tree trunk or rock formation. In the Lower Yukon Delta region, meandering was a constant problem. In addition, on the lower end of the river, the tides affected the river's water level and a poor channel choice might result in a boat reaching a dead end or the river lowering, leaving it stranded on high ground.

One constant problem was sandbars. Their presence could always be expected, but their location moved according to the river's fluid nature. When a boat ran aground on a sandbar, steamer crews worked tirelessly to get their boats free, using a variety of methods. One of the easiest methods of extraction from a sandbar was to back up the boat intermittently with as much force of the paddle wheel as possible, with the wheel washing away the sandbar. With the shifting sands and gravel, the boat might be able to cross over the bar and back into the river's current.

If that failed, two other techniques—"lining" and "sparring"— could be tried. The lining approach was to simply attach a cable wire from the boat to a well-anchored object—such as a tree—along the river's banks called a "dead man." The boat end of the line was attached to the steamer's capstan, a horizontal wheel on the main deck. The capstan was turned, with the wire winding up on the capstan, and the boat was winched off the sandbar. Sparring was a bit more complicated and tricky. The technique required two giant spars or wooden "legs," which were swung out into the water at a 45-degree angle. Blocks were attached to the spar tops along with ropes, again connected to the capstan. As the spar "feet" dug into the sandbar, the ropes were tightened, drawing the boat off the sandbar—similar to a skier using poles to push forward. This complicated technique was also referred to as "grass-hoppering." Sometimes, boat pilots relied on a combination of both lining and sparring. If all other methods failed to remove the boat from a sandbar, the paddle wheeler might have its cargo off-loaded, along with its passengers, relieving the boat of considerable tonnage, lightening the craft, and perhaps allowing the stranded vessel to slide off the natural obstacle.

DECADES OF SERVICE ON THE YUKON

During the days of the Klondike gold rush (1896–1898), perhaps as many as 100 paddle wheelers saw service on the Yukon River. In truth, those final years before 1900 were the busiest for steamer traffic on the great northern river. Even after the decline of the gold-rush era, though, steamboating remained an important form of transportation in Alaska and Yukon Territory. Paddle wheelers remained in use even after rail service reached Whitehorse in 1900, hauling equipment and supplies, as well as passengers. Several shipping companies operated on the river in the early twentieth century, but lower profits often resulted in steamboat service becoming less reliable, as "shipments were split up; custom papers were lost; supplies were stolen and the boats were unsafe."[77]

DREADING THE THIRTY MILE

Veteran steamboat pilots on the Yukon knew from years of experience that they could never take the river and its many obstacles and dangers for granted. Every mile of the great northern river featured its own hazards, but riverboat pilots held a special dread for a section of the Upper Yukon called the "Thirty Mile."

This section lies in the Canadian portion of the Yukon, between Lake Laberge and Hootalinqua. For the paddle wheelers of the late nineteenth century, the stretch between the gold camp towns of Whitehorse and Dawson was the most feared. Here, the Yukon is a narrow river, fast moving and very twisted. Flowing out of Lake Laberge, the water is clear but shallow, revealing dangers and challenges to a riverboat pilot:

> Because the Thirty Mile is so shallow, the boater may glimpse bed gravels, which will appear to be coming at him like snowflakes viewed through a moving car's windshield. Riffles make navigation interesting, as do the sharp bends and eddies. High banks of exposed sediments, while not uncommon elsewhere on the Yukon, are especially dominant on the narrow Thirty Mile. A strong wind sweeping across the face of the cutbank at Cape Horn is likely to stir fine sediments into billowing clouds that swirl high above the bank.[*]

Perhaps some of the first non-Indians to attempt a passage along the Thirty Mile included a team of prospectors led by Edward Bean in 1880. Three years later, Lt. Frederick Schwatka and his exploratory party took their raft through the Thirty Mile, where they worked desperately to keep their "ponderous raft from grounding on bars or colliding with the shoreline."[**] In his diary, Schwatka noted the experience of his Thirty Mile river run:

As early as 1901, the White Pass Company, the narrow-gauge rail line that ran in Whitehorse, became so disappointed with the generally poor steamboat service that its owners bought four boats—the *Canadian, Columbian, Sybil,* and *Yukoner*—from the Canadian Development Company and signed

On the 9th of July we passed out of Kluk-Tas-Si [native name for Laberge]. In this part of the river we usually grounded once or twice a day on sand, mud or gravel bars, and I think I have given them in the inverse order of the difficulty experienced in getting off them, sand being the worst and gravel the easiest from which the raft ban be liberated.***

To many steamboat pilots who navigated the waters of the Thirty Mile during the days of the paddle wheelers, the Thirty Mile was the most difficult leg between Whitehorse and Dawson. The passage through these waters usually took five hours downstream and about seven hours upstream. Wrecks along the dreaded passage were common. According to one eye-witness, "30 mile was so treacherous that it was lined with wrecks for all of its brief length; on July 8 the remains of nineteen boats were counted on a single rock in the main channel."†

Today, nearly a half-century after the end of the era of the paddle wheelers on the Yukon, Thirty Mile is still a notable stretch of the river but for another reason. Modern-day canoeists are drawn to the river's once notorious leg because it is one of the most scenic portions of the river. Hundreds of vacationing canoe adventurers paddle the spectacular waters between Whitehorse and Dawson each summer, passing by a nearly century-old reminder of the dangers that Thirty Mile once represented to paddle wheelers—the skeletal remains of the wreck of the *Casca*, a steamboat that went down after striking a rock in the river during a run in the summer of 1909.

 * The Upper Yukon Basin, *Alaska Geographic* 14(4):72, 1987.
 ** Ibid., 73.
 *** Ibid., 73.
  † Ibid., 73.

contracts for building new boats under its management. Soon, the rail line and steamboat service were operating under the same banner, allowing the White Pass Company to reduce its fares and provide better service from Skagway to Dawson.

Steamboats docked on the Yukon River in Ruby, Alaska. By the turn of the twentieth century, steamboats had become the preferred mode of transportation in the Yukon River region. Even after the gold rush came to an end, steamboats remained important in hauling equipment and supplies, as well as passengers.

The White Pass Company's steamboat line was known as the British Yukon Navigation Company, and its steamers plied the waters of the Yukon between Whitehorse and Dawson. The British Yukon Navigation Company also operated boats on Tagish and Atlin Lakes. Another company, the Side Stream Navigation Company, provided supplemental service for the British Yukon Navigation Company between 1909 and 1919, operating a small fleet of shallow draft paddle wheelers on various tributaries of the Yukon, such as the Pelly, Porcupine, Stewart, and White. Its boats included the *Nasutlin, Pauline,* and *Vidette.*

By 1913, the White Pass Company began operation of another steamboat line, the Alaska Yukon Navigation Company, which operated boats on the Lower Yukon from Dawson to St. Michael, located hundreds of miles downstream at the river's mouth. The company also provided service on additional Yukon tributaries downriver, including the Iditarod, Koyukuk, and Tanana Rivers. The following year, it purchased a rival steamboat service, the Northern Navigation Company, in an effort to end some of the cutthroat competition between the two steamboat lines. Ten years later, as the need for steamboat service dwindled, the Alaska Yukon Navigation Company only operated one boat, the *Yukon*, and by 1942, the company went completely out of business.

One incentive for keeping steamboats on the Yukon in operation even after the Klondike Gold Rush was the still-active mining industry in the region. Although much of the surface gold had been removed by tens of thousands of placer miners in just a few years, there were still gold and silver deposits underground. In 1915, a silver-lead ore strike along the Stewart River, a tributary of the Yukon, provided business for both the White Pass Company and others. As corporate mining developed, with its extensive underground shaft operations, the steamboats hauled in heavy mining equipment. Ore was also shipped by paddle wheelers from the mining camps, floated to Whitehorse, and shipped by rail to Skagway. Ore transport on Yukon steamers continued until the early 1950s, when highway construction in the region allowed for overland truck shipping.

THE END OF THE PADDLE-WHEELER ERA

Throughout the decades of operation along the Yukon River, approximately 250 paddle wheelers traversed its waters at one time or another. Although steamboats could still be seen in service on the Yukon as late as the 1960s and 1970s, the heyday for the steamers was the Klondike gold rush years of the late nineteenth century. During that time, paddle wheelers carried tens of thousands of prospectors and other fortune seekers into the subarctic north. When the gold began to disappear, the steamboat lost its usefulness. However, as long as steamboats continued to travel along the Yukon, from its mouth to its headwaters, the settlements on the river, from St. Michael to Dawson, remained viable and reasonably prosperous.

During the early twentieth century, other means of transportation reduced the importance of riverboat navigation. Many communities along the Yukon River therefore experienced "bust-and-boom" cycles, and many former mining towns and settlements simply vanished into ghost towns. When the 1,100-mile-long White Pass and Yukon Railways reached the Upper Yukon region in 1900, connecting the port of Skagway with Whitehorse and the Yukon River, paddleboats lost their importance. Lower Yukon towns, disconnected from their Upper Yukon counterparts because of the declining steamer traffic, lost their importance.

With the gold rush over, the Klondike region of the Yukon Valley became depopulated and many paddle wheelers were simply beached, unable to make a profit. For some tenacious owners, paddle wheeling continued, but "the economic base was unable to support many ships."[78] New modes of transportation reached Alaska during the twentieth century with the building of the Alaska Railway in 1923, which linked Valdez, Fairbanks, and Nenana. By the 1920s, commercial airlines and privately owned bush planes began providing services once virtually monopolized by the steamboats of earlier decades. Then, in 1942, the Alcan (Alaska) Highway was completed and its extension from Whitehorse to Dawson Creek, British Columbia, represented "the final nail in the coffin"[79] for steamboating. The few remaining paddle wheelers were occasionally used to carry supplies and U.S. Army personnel to various government bases.

8

Epilogue

Although Yukon Valley mining towns such as Circle City have dwindled in population and overall historical significance since the gold rush days of more than a century ago, other Yukon towns have retained their importance. Whitehorse, located along the headwaters of the Yukon, became the site of copper strikes by 1897, just as word of the Klondike gold rush was beginning to reach the outside world. One miner, Jack McIntyre, staked his first claim the following year and soon became known as the Copper King. Between 1902 and 1909, the Canadian government in Yukon Territory spent almost $50,000 building 36 miles of road through the region. Also, by 1909, the White Pass and Yukon Railways, the narrow-gauge rail line running from Skagway to Whitehorse, where navigation on the Yukon River had historically been located, built a spur railroad line to the copper mines. Copper mining, though, never drew the great number of miners that earlier gold strikes had produced, but mining in the region did continue until the 1980s.

Because of various mining enterprises throughout the Upper Yukon region during the first half of the twentieth century, Whitehorse remained an important river town of the north. By the spring of 1900, the town included several stores, six large hotels, two drugstores, a brickyard, warehouses along the waterfront, three churches, an athletic club, and an electricity-generating facility.

In 1920, airplanes brought new residents into the Yukon Valley for the first time in the twentieth century. That year, four de Havilland DH-4 biplanes of the First Alaska Air Expedition reached the Yukon during a flight from New York to Nome, on the western coast of Alaska. The entire flight took a month; it began on July 15, 1920, from the Hudson River Palisades. The planes, sporting 400-horsepower Liberty motors, flew at a top speed of 115 miles per hour. The eight men on board the de Havilland DH-4 biplanes were U.S. Army

During the Klondike gold rush, Whitehorse was a jumping off point for prospectors. The White Pass and Yukon Route Railway connected Skagway, Alaska, with Whitehorse, and the Yukon River connected Whitehorse to the gold fields around Dawson City. Whitehorse became the capital of Yukon Territory in 1953 and remains a center of transportation today.

pilots who hopped and skipped their planes across the northern United States, making frequent stops along the way, until they reached Canadian air space. The planes landed outside Whitehorse on August 16. The entire trip from New York had covered "nine thousand miles in 112 hours of flying, with the same airplanes, same motors, and same spark-plugs."[80] The four biplanes also landed at other Yukon Valley towns, including Dawson City, Fairbanks, and Ruby, "enchanting many Yukoners with the prospect of future aviation."[81]

Aviation in the Yukon region soon became a popular mode of subarctic travel. The Canadian post office supported the expansion of airplanes in the region, allowing private companies to print and issue their own stamps for mail carried on their planes. The stamps were sometimes attached to the backs of envelopes, instead of on the front, like regular postage. One of the first commercial airlines serving the Yukon region was the Yukon Airways and Exploration Company, which was headquartered in Whitehorse. It made its first commercial airmail fight along the Yukon on November 11, 1927. The first plane was the *Queen of the Yukon*, which was from the same company that had built an identical plane made famous by Charles Lindbergh—the *Spirit of St. Louis*.

The 1930s saw the dawning of a new age of aviation across Alaska, including the Yukon River valley. By 1931, 22 planes had flown the skies of Yukon Territory and Alaska, and the number jumped to 42 just two years later. Used to deliver mail, some freight, and passengers, these planes "flew more than a million passenger-miles and carried more than 700,000 pounds of freight and mail."[82]

By the early 1940s, the impact of World War II was felt all the way to the Yukon River, when the U.S. government leased the White Pass and Yukon Railway to carry supplies to military bases in western Alaska. During 1943 alone, the U.S. Army moved nearly 300,000 tons of freight for the war effort, more than the railroad had shipped during the previous 10 years. Following the war, Whitehorse continued to grow in population and importance, with the population doubling between 1941 and 1951. The Royal Canadian Mounted Police established the Yukon Subdivision Headquarters in Whitehorse in 1943. By the early 1950s, Whitehorse was the new capital of Yukon Territory. Later in the decade, a hydroelectric plant was constructed along the Upper Yukon at Whitehorse Rapids, providing additional electrical power for the region. By the 1960s and 1970s, tourism became one of Whitehorse's most important economic resources. In 1966, one of Whitehorse's most popular tourist attractions—the SS *Klondike* National Historic Site—was installed in the town by Parks Canada. The highlight of the attraction for tourists is a permanently docked paddle-wheel steamer. The SS *Klondike* served the towns along the Yukon from 1937 until the 1950s.

Other Yukon region towns that sprang up during the late-nineteenth-century gold rush days also remain vibrant commercial and residential centers today. In the midst of the 1898 Klondike gold rush, Dawson City had been the largest Canadian town west of Winnipeg, with 40,000 people walking its muddy streets. By the following year, 8,000 people left Dawson during the summer alone. By 1902, Dawson had dwindled to 5,000 but remained the seat of the territorial government. Large-scale corporate mining in the region around Dawson came to an end after the Klondike placer strikes, but the surface gold rush took several decades to completely run its course, peaking through high-volume machine mining in 1911. During the 1930s, Dawson City experienced a revival of its gold rush heyday as higher gold prices served as a new incentive to mine for gold. Not until 1966 was the last gold dredge of a long golden period in Yukon history finally shut down, but a new wave of higher gold prices has managed to reopen some mining districts.

With the arrival of the Alaska Highway in Whitehorse during the 1940s, and the end of steamboat travel into the region by the 1950s, Dawson declined further. Today, Dawson is home to approximately 2,000 permanent residents—but 60,000 tourists visit the town annually, drawn by the historic buildings and Canada's only legalized gambling house, bar, and cancan show: "Diamond Tooth Gertie's Gambling Hall,"

Five Finger Rapids, located near Carmacks, Yukon Territory, about halfway between Dawson City and Whitehorse, was once a treacherous stretch of river for steamboat captains to navigate. Today, the area is a popular destination for outdoor enthusiasts.

a highlight of each summer's tourist season. (Diamond Tooth Gertie was a famous dance-hall proprietress during the Klondike gold rush.)

Overall, the number of tourists who reach the Yukon every summer sometimes reaches into the hundreds of thousands; vacationing adventurers lured by the excellent fishing, hunting, canoeing, kayaking, hiking, and climbing offered by the Yukon

River, as well as its adjacent streams, forests, rock formations, mountains, and meadowlands. The increase in tourism to the Yukon Valley, as well as the development of the Arctic oil fields of Alaska's North Slope, have caused an increase in highway construction, all designed to "tap resources north of the Yukon River."[83] Canada began construction on the Dempster Highway in 1957 to aid in discovering more northern oil and gas fields.

After the 1968 discovery of oil at Prudhoe Bay, the road was further developed by 450 miles from Dawson northward to the mouth of the Mackenzie River, but it was not completed and opened to the public until 1979. The great Alaska Oil Pipeline necessitated the building of yet another road from Fairbanks during those years, and this included the construction of the only bridge spanning the Yukon River. The bridge was erected on giant pylons set hundreds of feet into the Yukon's river bottom to help it withstand the mighty floes of ice that crash down the river during the annual spring melt.

Because the Yukon River has remained one of western Canada's and Alaska's greatest natural resources, the United States and Canadian governments have sought to preserve as much of the area around the river as possible. Environmental and conservation efforts have become more important; one such effort resulted in the creation of the Yukon-Charley Rivers National Preserve during the mid-1970s. It is located along the Canadian border in central Alaska and includes 160 miles of the Yukon River basin, as well as the entire length of the Charley River, one of the Yukon's tributaries, which meanders for 100 miles from its headwaters to the Yukon. For many canoeists and kayakers, the Charley is one of the grandest, most beautiful rivers in Alaska. Along this stretch of the Yukon, the river is lined with stark reminders of the 1898 gold rush, including rustic log cabins and other historic sites. Archaeologists and paleontologists have studied the river lands within the Yukon-Charley Preserve and have uncovered evidence that humans have lived there for thousands of years. Today, the preserve is intended to help sustain the region's natural environment.

Within the 2.5-million-acre preserve, as well as along most stretches of the Yukon River, nature continues to flourish and run free, as it has for countless millennia. The wildlife in the rolling hills that flank these rivers is abundant, and includes wolves, bears, caribou, and moose. Near Fortymile, a caribou herd migrates annually through the Yukon-Charley River basin. Above these waterways, along the high bluffs that line the river, peregrine falcons continue to make their nests and raise their young undisturbed. Perhaps 20 percent of the peregrine population of North America is located within the Yukon-Charley Preserve.

Although the Yukon-Charley Preserve has been established to conserve a portion of the Yukon in its natural state, much of the remainder of the river remains vulnerable. Fortunately, the number of people who reside along the river remains relatively low, keeping the overall human impact on the great river to a minimum. Though the search for gold no longer influences the amount of traffic that traverses the river, the Yukon of the twenty-first century remains vital to the future of both Alaska and Yukon Territory. Its waters still originate from crystalline snows that are pure and unpolluted. The river remains so clean that it provides endless recreation for tens of thousands.

To date, no extensive damming system has been placed on the great northern river to impede its natural flow. During the 1960s, plans were developed for the construction of a massive dam at Rampart, Alaska, which would have backed up the flow of the Yukon River for close to 300 miles—nearly to the Canadian border. Although such a dam would have been one of the largest ever constructed in the world, the project was scrapped decades ago but pressure to build one has never ceased. Such a dam "would destroy significant fisheries, waterfowl nesting, wildlife habitat, and several Native villages. The Yukon could never recover." [84]

Today, Alaskans and Canadians of the twenty-first century remain the keepers of the river; they must work to preserve it. The Yukon remains, for all of us, the primary river of North America's final frontier and a window into our past.

1 MILLION B.P. Immense ice sheet begins to move and shift
(BEFORE PRESENT) across the region of northwestern Canada and
Alaska, scarring the land for hundreds of thousands
of years and creating the valleys that today constitute
the Yukon River system.

20000 B.C. The ice bridge between Siberia and Alaska allows
animals and humans to migrate into the Yukon
region from Asia.

6000 B.C. Early Athapaskans arrive in the Yukon region.

A.D. 1741 Sailing for the Russians, Danish sea captain Vitus
Bering discovers the Alaskan Coast.

1790s Russian fur trade in Alaska is among the most
lucrative trade in the world.

1829 Russians reach the mouth of the Yukon River.

1 million B.P.
(before present)
Yukon River
system created

20000 B.C.
Humans migrate to the
Yukon region from Asia

1878
George Holt discovers gold at the
headwaters of the Yukon River

1867
United States purchases
Alaska from Russia

1848
Robert Campbell establishes Fort Selkirk

1 MILLION B.P. **1800** **1900**

6000 B.C.
Athapaskans arrive
in the Yukon region

1829
Russians reach
the mouth of
the Yukon River

1896
The Klondike gold rush begins
after George Carmack, Tagish
Charlie, and Skookum Jim find
gold along Rabbit Creek

A.D. 1741
Vitus Bering discovers
the Alaskan Coast

1900
More than 200 steamboats
traversed the waters of the Yukon

1834 Russian explorer Andree Glazanoff reaches the confluence of the Yukon and Anvik Rivers.

1841–1842 Robert Campbell develops the Hudson's Bay Company trade out of Fort Hackett and establishes a post at Frances Lake.

1847 Alexander Hunter Murray, agent of the Hudson's Bay Company, establishes Fort Yukon on the river.

1848 Robert Campbell establishes a post at the confluence of the Pelly and Lewes Rivers, called Fort Selkirk, the first trading post built on the upper end of the Yukon River.

1866 Men laying the Russian-American Telegraph Company line deliver a small steamboat to the Yukon, named the *Wilder*.

1867 U.S. government purchases Alaska from the Russians.

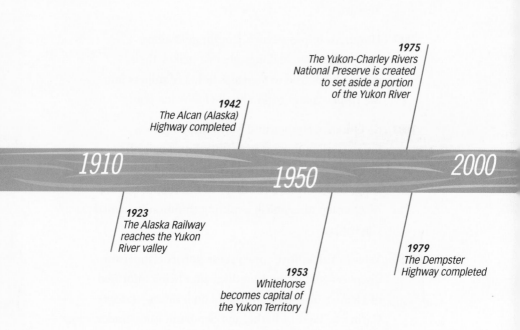

1975
The Yukon-Charley Rivers National Preserve is created to set aside a portion of the Yukon River

1942
The Alcan (Alaska) Highway completed

1910

1950

2000

1923
The Alaska Railway reaches the Yukon River valley

1953
Whitehorse becomes capital of the Yukon Territory

1979
The Dempster Highway completed

1869   Early rumors of gold discoveries in Alaska lure prospectors north.

1874   Employees of the Alaska Commercial Company, Leroy Napoleon "Jack" McQuesten and Arthur Harper, open a trading post—Fort Reliance—on the Yukon River.

1878   Prospector George Holt discovers gold at the headwaters of the Yukon River.

1883   Alfred Mayo partners with McQuesten and Harper; U.S. Army First Lieutenant Frederick Schwatka renames the Lewes River the Upper Yukon.

1884   A group of prospectors discover $100,000 in gold along the Upper Yukon River.

1886   McQuesten, Harper, and Mayo establish a new trading post at the mouth of the Stewart River; prospectors discover $100,000 in gold along the Stewart.

1887   Hundreds of prospectors pan for gold along Fortymile River, making valuable strikes; their success helps lead to a greater influx of miners into the Upper Yukon region by the following year.

1893   McQuesten, Harper, and Mayo break up their long-standing three-way partnership; a pair of prospectors employed by McQuesten find gold along Birch Creek, a tributary of the Yukon, leading McQuesten to establish a mining community named Circle City.

1896   Veteran Yukon River prospector Robert Henderson discovers gold in the Klondike; after being informed of Henderson's strike, three Yukon hunters—George Carmack, Tagish Charlie, and Skookum Jim—find a

bonanza of gold along Rabbit Creek, a tributary of
the Klondike; these discoveries lead to the great
Klondike gold rush of 1898; Rabbit Creek is
renamed Bonanza Creek.

1897   McQuesten is the wealthiest man in Circle City, as
local miners pan and dig out $1 million in gold;
trader Joe Ladue establishes the Klondike mining
community of Dawson City; 30 new steamboat
companies are doing business along the Yukon River.

1898   The Geographic Board of Canada votes to ignore
U.S. Army First Lieutenant Frederick Schwatka's
renaming of the Lewes River as the Upper Yukon
River; in the spring, tens of thousands of miners
reach the Klondike region; 110 paddle-wheel
steamboats are plying the Lower Yukon River.

1900   The number of steamboats on the Yukon exceeds
200; much of the Klondike Gold Rush has played
out; the White Pass and Yukon Railway reaches
the Upper Yukon region, connecting Skagway
with Whitehorse.

1923   The Alaska Railway reaches the Yukon River Valley.

1931   Twenty-two planes fly the skies of Yukon
Territory and Alaska; by 1933, the number has
nearly doubled.

1942   The Alcan (Alaska) Highway is completed, connecting Whitehorse to Dawson Creek, British Columbia.

1949   The Geographic Board of Canada officially renames
the Lewes River as the upper reaches of the Yukon
River.

1953   Whitehorse becomes the territorial capital of
Yukon Territory.

1960s Plans are discussed concerning a massive water impoundment project, the Rampart Dam, on the Yukon River; the controversy over the dam ensures that the project will not be built.

1975 The Yukon-Charley Rivers National Preserve is created to set aside a portion of the Yukon River and the entire length of the Charley to protect the rivers and their natural habitats.

1979 The Dempster Highway, linking Dawson to Inuvik, is completed.

CHAPTER 1:
The Great Northern River

1 Harry Ritter, *Alaska's History: The People, Land, and Events of the North Country* (Anchorage, Alaska: Alaska Northwest Books, 1993), 66.

2 Marian T. Place, *The Yukon* (New York: Ives Washburn, 1967), 9.

3 Ibid., 10.

4 Ibid., 15.

5 Ibid., 17.

6 Ibid., 18.

CHAPTER 2:
The People of the River

7 Alvin M. Josephy, Jr., *The Indian Heritage of America* (Boston, Mass.: Houghton Mifflin, 1991), 65.

8 Ibid., 67.

9 Ritter, *Alaska's History*, 25.

10 Ibid., 25.

11 Barry M. Pritzker, *A Native American Encyclopedia: History, Culture, and Peoples* (New York: Oxford University Press, 2000), 503.

12 Ritter, *Alaska's History*, 25.

13 Pritzker, *A Native American Encyclopedia*, 502.

14 Ibid., 506.

15 Josephy, *The Indian Heritage of America*, 69.

16 Ibid., 69.

17 Ibid., 71.

18 Place, *The Yukon*, 21.

19 Ibid., 22.

20 Ibid., 25.

21 Ibid., 26.

22 Ibid., 27.

23 Colin Taylor, *The American Indian* (London: Salamander Books, 2003), 216.

24 Ibid., 216.

25 Ibid., 215.

26 Ibid., 216.

CHAPTER 3:
Trade Rivals along the Yukon

27 Ritter, *Alaska's History*, 33.

28 Place, *The Yukon*, 36.

29 Ibid., 37.

30 Ibid., 38.

31 Ibid., 40.

32 Ibid., 41.

33 Ibid., 41.

34 Ibid., 42.

CHAPTER 4:
The Explorations of Robert Campbell

35 Place, *The Yukon*, 44.

36 Ibid., 45.

37 Ibid., 47.

38 Ibid., 48.

39 Ibid., 48.

40 Place, *The Yukon*, 51.

41 Ibid., 51.

42 Ibid., 52.

43 Ibid., 53.

CHAPTER 5:
Gold Rush along the Yukon

44 Place, *The Yukon*, 66.

45 Ibid., 71.

46 Pierre Berton, *The Klondike Fever: The Life and Death of the Last Great Gold Rush* (New York: Alfred A. Knopf, 1958), 12.

47 Michael Gates, *Gold at Fortymile Creek: Early Days in the Yukon* (Vancouver, B.C.: UBC Press, 1994), 21.

48 Berton, *The Klondike Fever*, 15.

49 Ibid., 19.

50 Place, *The Yukon*, 76–77.

51 Keith Wheeler, *The Alaskans* (Alexandria, Va.: Time-Life Books, 1977), 178.

52 Gates, *Gold at Fortymile Creek*, 40.

53 Ibid., 40.

54 Berton, *The Klondike Fever*, 22.

55 Ibid., 22.

56 Ibid., 28.

57 Ibid., 30.

58 Ibid., 29.

59 Ibid., 33.

60 Ibid., 31.
61 Ibid., 31.

CHAPTER 6:
The Klondike Gold Rush

62 Berton, *The Klondike Fever*, 34.
63 Ibid., 38.
64 Ibid., 47.
65 Wheeler, *The Alaskans*, 138.
66 Berton, *The Klondike Fever*, 47.
67 Place, *The Yukon*, 89.
68 Berton, *The Klondike Fever*, 51.
69 Ibid., 52.
70 Graham Wilson, *Paddlewheelers of Alaska and the Yukon* (Whitehorse, Yukon Territory: Wolf Creek Books, 1999), 9.
71 Michael Cooper, *Klondike Fever: The Famous Gold Rush of 1898* (New York: Clarion Books, 1989), 15.
72 Ibid., 21.
73 Berton, *The Klondike Fever*, 147.
74 Cooper, *Klondike Fever*, 28.

CHAPTER 7:
Paddle Wheelers on the Yukon

75 Wilson, *Paddlewheelers of Alaska and the Yukon*, 29.
76 Stan Cohen, *Yukon River Steamboats* (Missoula, Mont.: Pictorial Histories Publishing, 1982), 61.
77 Cohen, *Yukon River Steamboats*, 10.
78 Wilson, *Paddlewheelers of Alaska and the Yukon*, 105.
79 Ibid., 105.

CHAPTER 8:
Epilogue

80 Place, *The Yukon*, 173.
81 Melody Webb, *Yukon: The Last Frontier* (Lincoln, Nebr.: University of Nebraska Press, 1985), 260.
82 Ira Harkey, *Pioneer Bush Pilot: The Story of Noel Wien* (Seattle, Wash.: University of Washington Press, 1974), 265.
83 Webb, *Yukon: The Last Frontier*, 258.
84 Ibid., 309.

Adney, Tappan. *Klondike Stampede.* New York: Harper Brothers, 1900.

Beck, Larry, et al. *Alaska and the Yukon.* New York: Facts on File Publications, 1983.

Berton, Pierre. *The Klondike Fever: The Life and Death of the Last Great Gold Rush.* New York: Alfred A. Knopf, 1958.

Breeden, Robert, ed. *Alaska: High Roads to Adventure.* Washington, D.C.: National Geographic Society, 1976.

Chevigny, Hector. *Russian America: The Great Alaskan Venture, 1741–1867.* New York: Viking Press, 1965.

Cohen, Stan. *Yukon River Steamboats.* Missoula, Mont.: Pictorial Histories Publishing, 1982.

Cooper, Michael. *Klondike Fever: The Famous Gold Rush of 1898.* New York: Clarion Books, 1989.

DeGraf, Anna. *Pioneering on the Yukon, 1892–1917.* Hamden, Conn.: Archon Books, 1992.

Dykstra, Monique. *My Heart on the Yukon River: Portraits from Alaska and the Yukon.* Pullman, Wash.: Washington State University Press, 1997.

Gates, Michael. *Gold at Fortymile Creek: Early Days in the Yukon.* Vancouver, B.C.: UBC Press, 1994.

Harkey, Ira. *Pioneer Bush Pilot: The Story of Noel Wien.* Seattle, Wash.: University of Washington Press, 1974.

Josephy, Alvin M., Jr. *The Indian Heritage of America.* Boston, Mass.: Houghton Mifflin, 1991.

Place, Marian T., *The Yukon.* New York: Ives Washburn, 1967.

Pritzker, Barry M. *A Native American Encyclopedia: History, Culture, and Peoples.* New York: Oxford University Press, 2000.

Ritter, Harry. *Alaska's History: The People, Land, and Events of the North Country.* Anchorage, Alaska: Alaska Northwest Books, 1993.

Satterfield, Archie. *Exploring the Yukon River.* Seattle, Wash.: The Mountaineers, 1979.

Shepherd, Donna Walsh. *Alaska.* New York: Children's Press, 1999.

BIBLIOGRAPHY

Sherwood, Morgan B. *Exploration of Alaska, 1865–1900.* New Haven, Conn.: Yale University Press, 1965.

Taylor, Colin. *The American Indian.* London: Salamander Books, 2003.

The Upper Yukon Basin. *Alaska Geographic.* Vol. 14, No. 4, 1987.

Webb, Melody. *Yukon: The Last Frontier.* Lincoln, Nebr.: University of Nebraska Press, 1985.

Wharton, David B. *The Alaska Gold Rush.* Bloomington, Ind.: Indiana University Press, 1972.

Wheeler, Keith. *The Alaskans.* Alexandria, Va.: Time-Life Books, 1977.

Wilson, Graham. *Paddlewheelers of Alaska and the Yukon.* Whitehorse, Yukon Territory: Wolf Creek Books, 1999.

Yardley, Joyce. *Yukon Riverboat Days.* Blaine, Wash.: Hancock House, 1996.

Haskell, William B., and Terrence Cole. *Two Years in the Klondike and Alaskan Gold Fields, 1896–1898*. Fairbanks, Alaska: University of Alaska Press, 1998.

Hildebrand, John. *Reading the River: A Voyage Down the Yukon*. Madison, Wisc.: University of Wisconsin Press, 1997.

London, Jack. *The Call of the Wild*. New York: Simon & Schuster Children's, 1999.

Murphy, Claire Rudolph. *Gold Rush Women*. Anchorage, Alaska: Alaska Northwest Books, 1997.

Sturgis, Kent. *Four Generations on the Yukon*. Kenmore, Wash.: Epicenter Press, Inc., 1990.

Wilson, Graham. *Last Great Gold Rush: A Klondike Reader*. Whitehorse, Yukon Territory: Wolf Creek Books, Inc., 2001.

———. *The Klondike Gold Rush: Photographs from 1896–1899*. Whitehorse, Yukon Territory: Wolf Creek Books, Inc., 1997.

WEBSITES

Canadian Council for Geographic Education/The Yukon River
http://www.ccge.org/ccge/english/teachingResources/rivers/ tr_rivers_yukonRiver.htm

The Thirtymile Section of the Yukon River
http://collections.ic.gc.ca/rivers/hp14.html

All about the Yukon River
http://www.explorenorth.com/library/weekly/aa100199.htm

Photos of the Yukon River and Riverboats
http://www.gvn.net/~mraffety/yukon.html

Ross River, Yukon Territory
http://www.rossriver.yk.net/

Dalton Highway, 3
Dawson, George M., 77
Dawson City, 6, 76–80, 87–88,
    109–110
Dead Horse Trail, 85
Dease Lake, 44–48
death, beliefs about, 20, 21, 22,
    30
Dempster Highway, 111
Diamond Tooth Gertie's Gambling
    Hall, 109–110
diet
    Ingalik, 18–19
    Inuit, 25–26, 27–28
    Kutchin, 22
dogs, 27, 28, 69–70
Doll ceremony, 21
drainage area, 2
Dyea Inlet, 60
Dyea Trail, 84, 85–86

Eagle, 4, 6–7
Eskimo malamutes, 28
Eskimos. *See* Inuit tribe
ethnic groups, 12
Europeans' arrival in Yukon region,
    32
Excelsior (vessel), 80

Feast of the Dead, 30
First Alaska Air Expedition,
    106–108
fish, as diet staple, 18–19, 22, 28
Five Finger Rapids, 110
flooding, 3
food. *See* diet
Fort Halkett, British Columbia,
    44–45
Fort Reliance, 5–6, 57, 58
Fort Selkirk, 5, 49, 52–53, 54
Fort Simpson, 44, 48
Fort Union (Montana), 36
Fort Yukon, 9, 37–39, 42, 52
Fortymile (mining community),
    66

Fortymile River, 6, 59, 60, 62–66
Forty-Rod Whiskey, 66
Frances Lake, 48, 49

geology of Yukon River system,
    11–12
Glazanoff, Andree, 34–35
gold dust as currency, 87–88
the Golden Stairs, 85
gold rush, 6. *See also* Klondike
    gold rush; Yukon River gold
    rush
guns, trade and, 39, 42

Han tribe, 15, 17, 21
Harper, Arthur, 57–62, 65, 67, 72
Henderson, Robert, 72
Holt, George, 57
Hootalinqua River, 57–58,
    100–101
"hothouse" period of Alaskan
    history, 11
housing
    Ingalik, 18
    Inuit, 24–25
    Kutchin, 21–22
Hudson's Bay Co.
    Dease Lake, 44–48
    Fort Selkirk, 5, 49, 52–53, 54
    Fort Yukon, 36–39, 42
    Youcon River, 50
hunting, 16, 19, 22, 26–28, 34, 40

ice fields, 11
igloos, 25
Indian River, 72–73
Ingalik tribe, 15, 17–21
Inuit tribe
    in Circle City, 8
    Ingaliks and, 17
    migration to Alaska, 12
    overview, 24–30
    photograph, 15
    Russians and, 35
Inviting-in Festival, 30

wealth redistribution, 19
weaponry, 16, 17, 27
whales, hunting, 27–28
Wheeler, Herbert, 96
whiskey, 66
Whitehorse, 5, 106, 107–109
White Pass and Yukon Railways,
   104, 106, 108
White Pass Chronicle (newspaper),
   75
White Pass Co., 100–103
White River, 5
wildlife
   caribou, 16, 23
   hunting, 16, 19, 22, 26–28, 34,
      40
   overview, 3, 8
   peregrine falcons, 112
   Pleistocene, 11–12
   in Yukon-Charley Preserve, 112
Williams, Tom, 60–62
Wilson, Graham, 93
World War II, 108

Youcon River. *See* Yukon River
yua (spirit), 28, 29
Yuchoo (great river), 50
The Yukon (Place), 7–8
Yukon Airways and Exploration
   Co., 108
Yukon-Charley Rivers National
   Preserve, 111–112

Yukon Flats, 8, 10, 67, 98
Yukon Indians, 48
yukonna, 2
Yukon River
   course in Alaska, 6–10
   course in Yukon Territory, 2–6
   geology of, 11–12
   source of, 50–51
Yukon River gold rush. *See also*
   Klondike gold rush; McQuesten,
   Leroy "Jack"
   Birch Creek, 67
   Chilkoot Pass, 61
   Circle City, 67–70
   Dyea Inlet, 60
   Fort Reliance, 57, 58
   Fortymile River, 59, 60, 62–66
   Harper and, 57–62, 65, 67, 72
   Lewes River and, 51
   precursor to, 56–57
   sluices, washing gold in, 63, 64
   Stewart River, 58–59
   Upper Yukon River, 58
   Williams and Bob, 60–62
   Yukon Flats, 67
Yukon Territory
   creation of, 89
   Dawson City, 6, 76–80, 87–88
   Fort Reliance, 5–6, 57, 58
   Fort Selkirk, 5, 49, 52–53, 54
   Whitehorse, 5, 106, 107–109
   Yukon River in, 2–6

page:

4: © CORBIS

7: © Bettmann/CORBIS

15: © Michael Maslan Historic
Photographs/CORBIS

27: © Peter Harholdt/CORBIS

33: © Bettmann/CORBIS

41: © Michael Maslan Historic
Photographs/CORBIS

45: © Museum of History &
Industry/CORBIS

49: © Museum of History &
Industry/CORBIS

64: © Bettmann/CORBIS

68: Library of Congress,
LC-USZ62-65228

75: © Richard Cummins/CORBIS

77: © Bettmann/CORBIS

86: © CORBIS

102: Library of Congress,
LC-USZ62-66467

107: © James Marshall/CORBIS

110: © Carol Havens/CORBIS

Cover: © Paul A. Souders/CORBIS

Frontis: Library of Congress American Memory Map Collection

ABOUT THE AUTHOR

TIM McNEESE is an Associate Professor of History at York College in York, Nebraska, where he is currently in his thirteenth year of instruction. Professor McNeese earned an Associate of Arts degree from York College, a Bachelor of Arts in history and political science from Harding University, and a Master of Arts in history from Southwest Missouri State University.

A prolific author of books for elementary, middle and high school, and college readers, McNeese has published more than 70 books and educational materials over the past 20 years, on everything from Indian mythology to the building of the Great Wall of China. His writing has earned him a citation in the library reference work, *Something about the Author*. His wife, Beverly, is an Assistant Professor of English at York College and the couple has two children, Noah and Summer. Readers are encouraged to contact Professor McNeese at tdmcneese@york.edu.